Heinemann Games Series

English PUZZLES

1

TEACHER'S RESOURCE BOOK

Doug Case

PHOTOCOPIABLE

REVISED EDITION IN THREE LEVELS

Heinemann Games Series

Titles in this series include:

TEACHER'S RESOURCE BOOKS		CLASS BOOKS	
Play Games with English 1	0 435 25016 7	**Play Games with English 1**	0 435 28060 0
Play Games with English 2	0 435 25017 5	**Play Games with English 2**	0 435 28062 7
Play Games with English 3	0 435 25018 3		
Word Games with English 1	0 435 25088 4	**Word Games with English 1**	0 435 28380 4
Word Games with English 2	0 435 25089 2	**Word Games with English 2**	0 435 28381 2
Word Games with English 3	0 435 25090 6	**Word Games with English 3**	0 435 28382 0
		Word Games with English Plus	0 435 28379 0
English Puzzles 1	0 435 25084 1	**English Puzzles 1**	0 435 28280 8
English Puzzles 2	0 435 25085 X	**English Puzzles 2**	0 435 28281 6
English Puzzles 3	0 435 25086 8	**English Puzzles 3**	0 435 28282 4
		English Puzzles 4	0 435 28283 2

Heinemann English Language Teaching
A division of Heinemann Publishers (Oxford) Ltd
Halley Court, Jordan Hill, Oxford OX2 8EJ

OXFORD MADRID ATHENS PARIS FLORENCE PRAGUE SÃO PAULO
CHICAGO MELBOURNE AUCKLAND SINGAPORE TOKYO GABORONE
JOHANNESBURG PORTSMOUTH (NH) IBADAN

ISBN 0 435 25084 1

First published 1994

Illustrated by
Plum Design

Cover designed by Martin Cox

Teacher's pages designed and typeset by VAP

Acknowledgements
Thanks to Brigitte Zacharian for her help in testing the puzzles in this series of books; to Michèle Cronick and Charlotte Covill for their deft and thoughtful editing of the original Student's Book edition; and to them all for many valuable suggestions.
Thanks also to Deborah Manning and Michael Boyd for their care in overseeing the publication of this Teacher's Resource Book edition.

Printed and bound in Great Britain by
Thomson Litho Limited, East Kilbride, Scotland.

95 96 97 98 10 9 8 7 6 5 4 3 2

Contents

INDEX 4
TEACHER'S INTRODUCTION 5 - 6
PUZZLES 7 - 71
Coloured pens 7
Vocabulary: Colours
Film titles 8
Plural nouns; numbers
Shopping accident 9
Vocabulary: Food and drink
American football 10
Numbers; family names
Find the words 11
Letters of the alphabet; a/an
Wind damage 12
Vocabulary: Shops and public buildings
Crossword pieces 13
The days of the week
Male and female 14
Vocabulary: Family members
Add a letter 15
General vocabulary
Names 16
First names (short and full forms)
Theatre posters 17
Singular and plural nouns
Do-it-yourself 18
Vocabulary: Rooms
At the cinema 19
Family members and other male and female persons
A different alphabet 20
Vocabulary: Public buildings; letters of the alphabet
Countries in code 21
Countries; telling the time
At home 22
Vocabulary: Furniture
Book titles 23
Prepositions of place
Verb crossword 24
Present simple (especially third person singular spelling)
Add two letters 25
General vocabulary
TV programmes 26
General vocabulary; reading comprehension
Jobs 27
Vocabulary: Jobs
Song titles 28
he/she; his/her; him/her
Badges 29
General vocabulary; reading comprehension
Verb backgammon 30
Verb infinitives
Fruit 31
Vocabulary: Fruit
Mistakes on the signpost 32
Spelling: ch/tch/k/ck
Pounds and pence 33
Numbers; British currency
Musical instruments 34
Vocabulary: Musical instruments
Write the clues 35
-ing form of verbs, especially spelling
Radio programmes 36
General vocabulary; reading comprehension
Fifteen records 37
'*s* = is/has/*possessive*
Round and round 38
General vocabulary
Letters or words? 39
Letters of the alphabet; pronunciation
Daily newspapers 40
Names of British newspapers
Add three letters 41
General vocabulary
Rhyming pairs 42
Pronunciation: Rhyming words
Olympic rings 43
Vocabulary: Sports
Computer keyboard 44
Ordinal numbers; letters of the alphabet
Animals 45
Vocabulary: Animals
Shapes and letters 46
Shapes; reading comprehension
More newspapers 47
Names of British newspapers
Radio stations 48
Numbers; reading comprehension
Past and present 49
Past simple (irregular verbs)
Books, books, books 50
General vocabulary; reading comprehension
Telegrams 51
Expressions of good wishes
Mixed vegetables 52
Vocabulary: Vegetables
Verb dice 53
Past simple (regular verbs)
Record store 54
Question-words; am/is/are
Hidden prepositions 55
Prepositions of place
The last word 56
Contractions (aren't, didn't, wasn't, *etc.)*
Pictures and opposites 57
Opposite adjectives; general vocabulary
Months jigsaw 58
The months of the year
Verb mini-crossword 59
Verb infinitives; pronunciation
Don't do it - it's unlucky! 60
Negative imperatives; prepositions of place
Calculator 61
Large numbers
Folding doors 62
Warning notices
Longer, shorter 63
General vocabulary
Identity parade 64
Past simple; ages
Find the family 65
Possessive adjectives
Clothes 66
Vocabulary: Clothes
Elvis's greatest hits 67
General vocabulary; reading comprehension
A + B = C 68
Compound nouns
Mistakes at the airport 69
Signs and notices; spelling
Famous dates 70
Dates; past simple
Longer, shorter, longer... 71
General vocabulary
SOLUTIONS 72 - 80

Index

a/an **11**
adjectives
- opposites **57**
- possessive **65**
ages **64**
airport signs **69**
alphabet **11, 20, 39, 44**
am/is/are **54**
animals **45**
article, indefinite **11**
badges **29**
books **23, 50**
clothes **66**
colours **7**
compound nouns **68**
contractions **56**
countries **21**
currency (British) **33**
dates **70**
days of the week **13**
-ed ending (verbs) **53**
family members **14, 19**
famous people **64, 70**
famous places **65**
female and male **14, 19**
films **8, 19**
food and drink **9**
fruit **31**
furniture **22**
good wishes **51**
he/she, his/her, him/her **28**
home
- furniture **22**
- rooms **18**

imperatives **60**
indefinite article **11**
infinitive of verbs **30, 59**
-ing ending (verbs) **35**
jobs **27**
letters of the alphabet **11, 20, 39, 44**
male and female **14, 19**
money (British) **33**
months **58**
musical instruments **34**
names
- family names **10**
- first names **16**
newspapers (British) **40, 47**
nouns
- compound **68**
- plural **8**
- singular and plural **17**
numbers **8, 10, 33, 48, 61**
- ordinal numbers **44**
opposites **57**
past simple
- irregular verbs **49, 64**
- regular verbs **53**
- regular and irregular verbs **70**
people (male and female) **14, 19**
plays (theatre) **17**
plural nouns **8, 17**
possessive adjectives **65**
possessive *'s* **37**
prepositions of place **23, 55, 60**
present simple **24**
pronunciation **42, 59**
proverbs **22, 31**

public buildings and shops **12, 20**
question-words **54**
radio programmes **36**
radio stations **48**
rhyming words **42**
rooms **18**
-s ending (verbs) **24**
's (*is/has*/possessive) **37**
shapes **46**
shops and public buildings **12, 20**
singular and plural nouns **17**
songs **28, 37, 54, 67**
spelling **69**
- *ch/tch/k/ck* **32**
- verbs (*-ed* ending) **53**
- verbs (*-ing* ending) **35**
- verbs (*-s* ending) **24**
sports **43**
superstitions **60**
telegrams **51**
telling the time **21**
TV programmes **26**
vegetables **52**
verbs
- contractions **56**
- imperative **60**
- infinitive **30, 59**
- *-ing* form **35**
- past simple (irregular) **49, 64**
- past simple (regular) **53**
- past simple (regular and irregular) **70**
- present simple **24**
warning signs **62**

Teacher's Introduction

English Puzzles is a set of Teacher's Resource Books at three levels: (1) Beginner, (2) Elementary, (3) Intermediate. Each book contains over sixty puzzles, which can be used by secondary school students and adult learners, in class, for homework or in a self-access centre.

The appeal of puzzles

Solving puzzles is an enjoyable and satisfying activity which demands reflection, reasoning and deduction - and there is particular pleasure to be derived from solving puzzles which involve manipulating or 'playing with' language. David Crystal has summed up this fascination as follows:

> Playing with words is a universal human activity, but it is particularly noticeable in the way literate societies have devised word games, based largely on the written language. People delight in pulling words apart and reconstituting them in a novel guise, arranging them into clever patterns, finding hidden meanings inside them, and trying to use them according to specially invented rules. Word puzzles and competitions are to be found in newspapers, at parties, in schools, on radio and television, and in all kinds of individual contexts - as when an adult completes a crossword, or a child plays a game of Hangman.
>
> David Crystal, *The Cambridge Encyclopedia of Language* (CUP, 1987).

Indeed, a visit to a typical newsagent's demonstrates this enduring popularity. The shelves usually display many periodicals devoted entirely to puzzles, such as (in Britain) *The Puzzler*, (in France) *Sport Cérébral*, (in Italy) *La Settimana Enigmatistica*, and so on.

This popularity is a solid foundation on which to base the use of puzzles in language learning.

Types of puzzles

Not all puzzles involve language, of course. For example:

- puzzles based purely on the manipulation of numbers,
- puzzles which are purely tests of visual acuity.

Such puzzles have a limited value in foreign language learning, and are not used in **English Puzzles**.

Among puzzles which *do* involve language, some are not particularly suitable for foreign language learning. For example:

- puzzles which operate at the level of the letter and can be 'solved' without the need to fully understand the clues or the solution (such as the 'My first is in "winter" but not in "spring" ' type).

Others are not particularly suitable for other reasons, at least in the early stages. For example:

- puzzles whose interest value depends on obscure words or obscure knowledge, or on complicated plays on words or visual puns demanding native-speaker familiarity with the language (such as 'Call my bluff' and 'Rebus' puzzles),
- very intricate 'logic puzzles', which, if genuinely challenging from the logic side, may exert a strong pressure for the necessary thinking and verbalizing to be in the first language.

Such puzzles are also not used in **English Puzzles.**

There are, however, many widely-known puzzle types which adapt well to the language learning context. For example:

- crosswords in various formats,
- anagrams and other re-arrangements of letters,
- codes and other 'distortions' of text,
- find-the-word grids and other ways of concealing words,
- riddles and puzzles based on jokes,
- puzzles involving sorting or categorizing.

These are the types of puzzles - as well as specially devised ones - which are used in **English Puzzles**.

The usefulness of puzzles in language learning

Puzzles are useful for language learners because the enjoyment, satisfaction, reflection and 'play' can focus learners' attention on the language in a concentrated but non-stressful way.

Puzzles are thus a helpful complement to exercises. Exercises are useful and necessary, of course. However, an exercise may be perceived as a 'test' and make learners feel guilty or inadequate if they are unable to get all the answers right. A puzzle involves less stress. Solvers do not necessarily *expect* to find every single answer, although they *hope* to do so. The solution may have to be consulted for one or two answers, but as long as the puzzle is perceived as fair and interesting, it remains an enjoyable activity.

Also, exercises often contain discrete items - separate sentences to be completed, for example. In a puzzle, finding one answer often helps the solver to find other answers, thus giving more scope for reasoning and deduction. And the learner's attitude towards encountering unknown words may be more positive in a puzzle than in an exercise: a degree of mystery is a part of the puzzle context, and unknown words may thus be less 'threatening'.

Puzzles are often described as 'light relief' from 'serious' learning. This rather undervalues their usefulness. It would be better to describe them as an enjoyable contribution to and reinforcement of learning.

Choosing puzzles from ENGLISH PUZZLES

The majority of the puzzles in **English Puzzles** focus on specific language areas. These language areas are grammatical points, lexical sets, spelling rules, aspects of pronunciation, functions, situations and styles (such as formal style, colloquial usage and politeness).

There are also some puzzles which combine several areas, and others which are intended to be generally accessible to the level in terms of their language content and the complexity of the reading comprehension task involved.

It is worth remembering that the puzzles are intended to be more than just illustrated exercises. Thus, a puzzle may be 'about' a particular language point without that point actually being manipulated. An example of this is the 'Special Sentences' puzzle in Book 2: the puzzle revolves around a set of sentences, in each of which the verb is in the Present Perfect tense, but in the context of the puzzle these sentences are 'special' for other reasons.

There are two ways in which you can identify puzzles you may wish to use with your students:

- In each book, the language area for each puzzle is given in the list of puzzles on the *Contents* page.
- Each book also contains an alphabetical *Index* of these language areas. The *Index* also includes 'topics' which occur in the puzzles (such as 'films', 'songs', 'books', 'superstitions', 'proverbs' or 'famous people'), since you may wish to choose a puzzle for its topic as well as for its language area.

Using the puzzles in ENGLISH PUZZLES

The puzzles are designed to be incorporated alongside the practice your students are doing with their main coursebook, just like any other type of supplementary material.

In the classroom, puzzles can be used in the way you would normally use written exercises or reading comprehension tasks. They can be done by students individually - all students having the same puzzle, or some students having one puzzle and some another - with students comparing their solutions and then a full-class check on the solutions.

Alternatively, they can be done by the students in pairs or in small groups. All groups may work on the same puzzle, or there may be several puzzles in use at the same time in different groups, with inter-group comparisons and full-class checking as above. Or each group may have a set of, say, three puzzles to solve (all groups having the same three puzzles), with an element of competition being introduced between the groups or against the clock.

With puzzles whose artwork is relatively easy to imitate by hand (those involving grids, such as crosswords, for example), you may like to reproduce the grid on the blackboard while the students are solving the puzzle, and use this blackboard grid in the checking of the solution.

Most of the puzzles are 'self-contained', i.e. the final aim is to arrive at the solution. Some, however, are accompanied by a question which can lead on to brief follow-up discussion if desired (e.g. 'Don't do it - it's unlucky!' in Book 1, or 'Twenty-one proverbs' in Book 3).

You may also like to use puzzles *for homework*, as they can provide an enjoyable supplement to exercises, reinforcing the language areas your students have been practising in class.

You may also find puzzles useful *in a self-access centre*, if your school has one. In this case, it would be useful to make the Indexes available to the users, so that they themselves can also locate the particular puzzles they may wish to do.

A word about puzzle instructions

In any language learning activity, it is of course important that the learners understand the instructions - and this is perhaps particularly true of puzzles. Thus, if there are any expressions in the instructions to a puzzle which you think your students will be unfamiliar with, clarify these before the solving begins!

Puzzle instructions sometimes contain specialised words ('grid' or 'clues', for example) or words used with special meanings (such as 'boxes'). The principal such words used in the instructions in **English Puzzles** are explained and illustrated on the two pages called *Puzzle Instructions* at the back of Book 2. You may find it useful to copy these pages, or relevant parts of them, for your students.

And finally, one very useful practical instruction is this: When solving puzzles, use a pencil and an eraser!

Coloured pens

In your imagination, pick up these pens one by one – taking the *top* one each time.

BRO N
B E
REY
GRE N
YE OW
BLACK
R
WH E
O ANGE
1 BLACK
2
3
4
5
6
7
8
9
B L A C K

Write the complete words for the colours here – in the correct order ......

.... and then put the words into the grid.

Film Titles

Read the film titles and write them on the correct posters. (The films are from the United Kingdom, the United States, France and Italy.)

- Two People (US, 1973)
- Two Women (IT/FR, 1960)
- Three Men In A Boat (UK, 1956)
- Three Men On A Horse (US, 1936)
- Seven Women (US, 1966)
- Seven Angry Men (US, 1954)
- Ten Tall Men (US, 1951)
- Twelve Angry Men (US, 1957)

1

2

3

4

5

6

7

8

PHOTOCOPIABLE

SHOPPING Accident

Write the complete words in the grid, vertically.
They make another word in the special squares, horizontally.

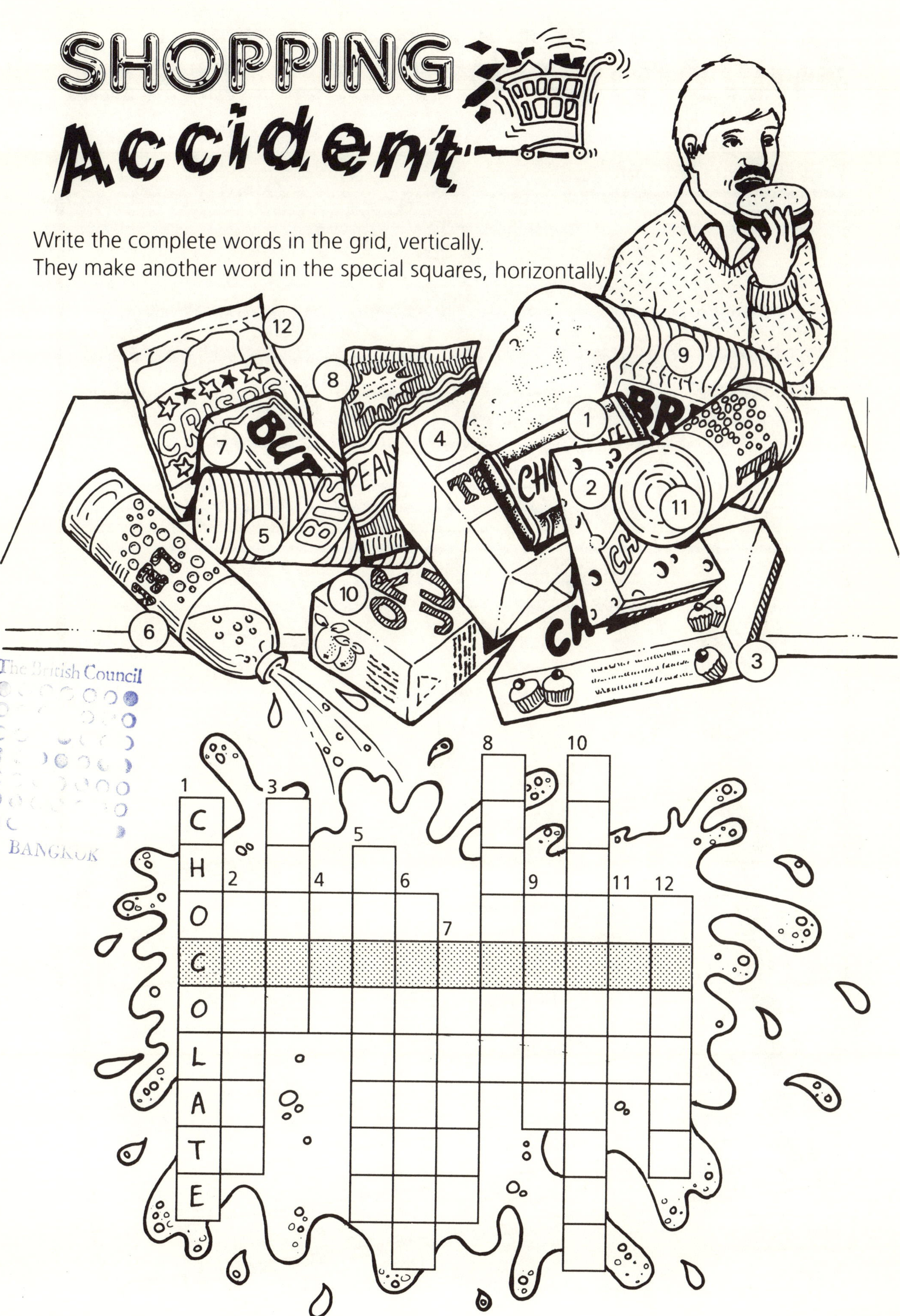

12
CRISPS
8
PEAN
9
BR
7
BUT
4
T
1
CHO
2
CH
11
5
BIS
6
10
OR
JU
CA
3
1 CHOCOLATE
2
3
4
5
6
7
8
9
10
11
12

HEINEMANN ENGLISH LANGUAGE TEACHING

AMERICAN FOOTBALL

Look at this picture of an American football match. What do you think the players' names are?

- Number One's name is
- Number Three's name is
- Number Seven's name is
- Number Twelve's name is
- Number Twenty-eight's name is
- Number Thirty-seven's name is
- Number Forty's name is
- Number Forty-one's name is

Question:

What is special about those names?

PHOTOCOPIABLE

Find the words

Find the words and write them in the correct boxes.
Put *a* or *an* with each word, like the examples.

A P P L E B O T T L E C
Y E R O O D E T T E S S A
E F I S H G L O V E H A N
A J T C E S N I R U O H D
C K E T K E Y L A M P M O
R O T S E N E K I B R O T
A N G E P L A N E Q U E U
C I W D N A S R E L U R E
H T A B L E U M B R E L L
I L O I V M R O F I N U A
N W A T C H X Y L O P H O
A R B E Z T H C A Y E N
B
C
a cassette
G
A
D
F
J
a jacket
E
M
N
K
L
H
60 MINS
H
I
P
Q
R
S
O
U
U
X
Z
W
V
Y
T

WIND DAMAGE

Some letters are missing from the buildings after a strong wind.
Can you replace them?

PHOTOCOPIABLE

Crossword Pieces

Assemble the pieces of the crossword onto the grid below, to see six days of the week.

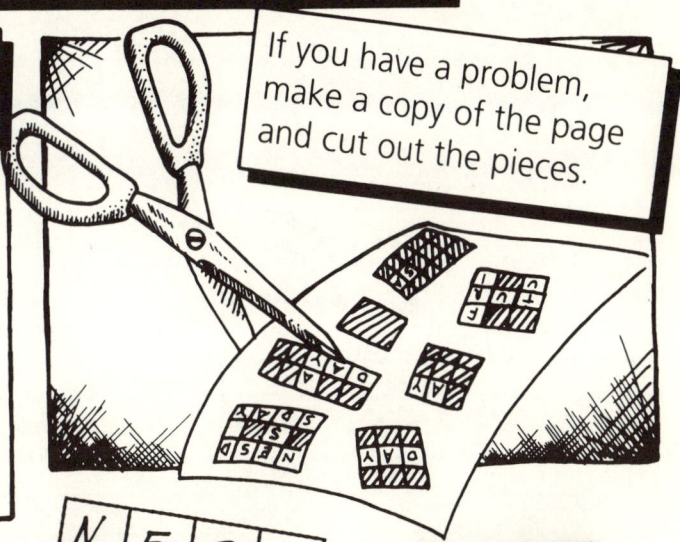

Do it in your head if you can.

If you have a problem, make a copy of the page and cut out the pieces.

One piece is already in position.

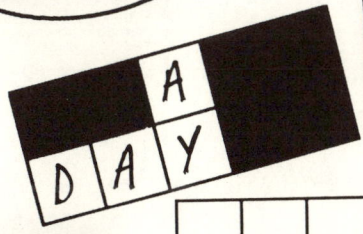

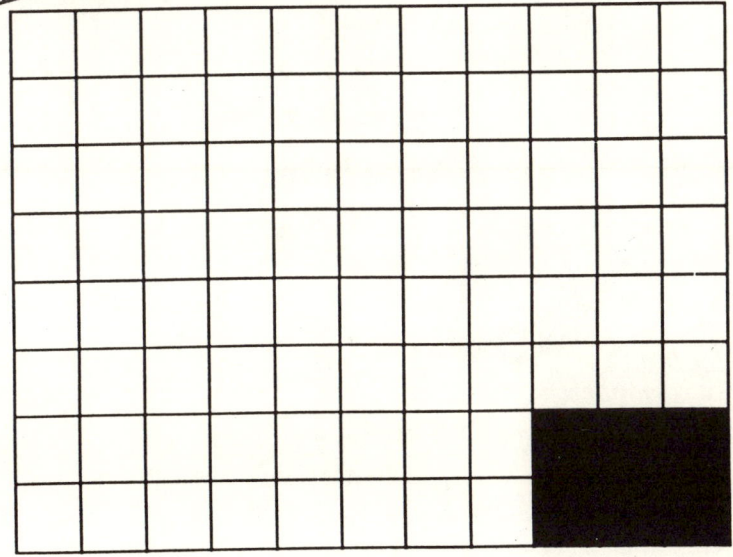

Question:
Which day is not in the crossword?

HEINEMANN ENGLISH LANGUAGE TEACHING

PHOTOCOPIABLE

Male and Female

Look at the two crosswords. In Crossword A, every answer is a word for a *male* person. Complete Crossword B: every answer is a word for a *female* person.

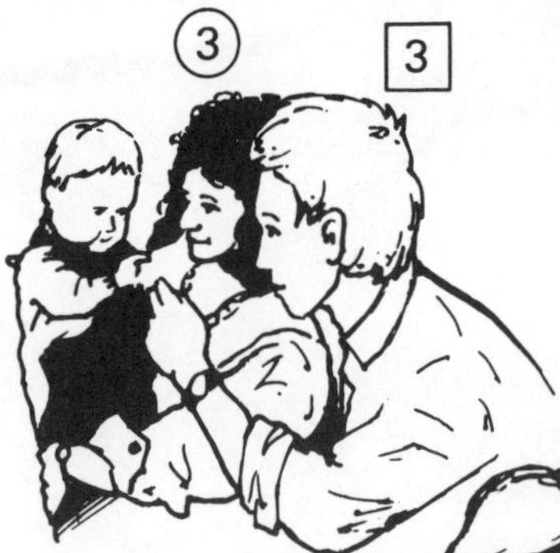

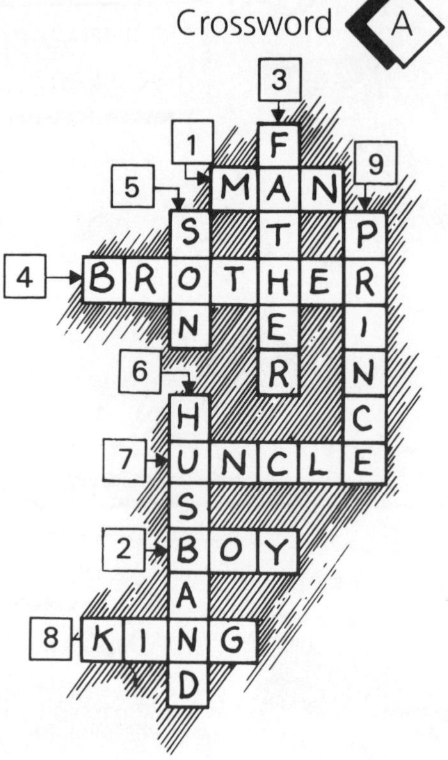

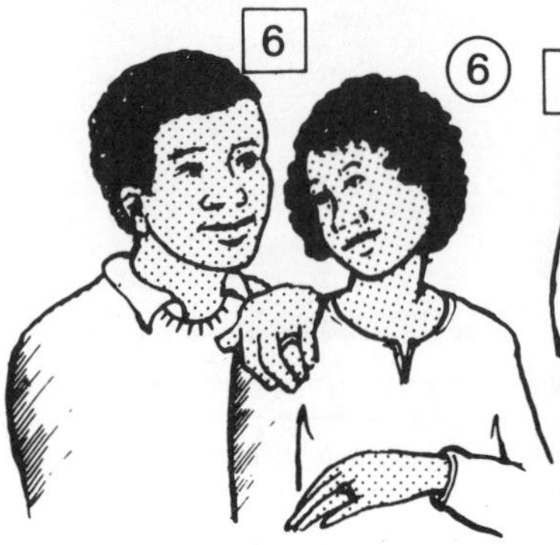

Crossword A

Crossword B

PHOTOCOPIABLE

Add a letter

Write the words on the left. Then add a letter to each word, to get the words on the right.

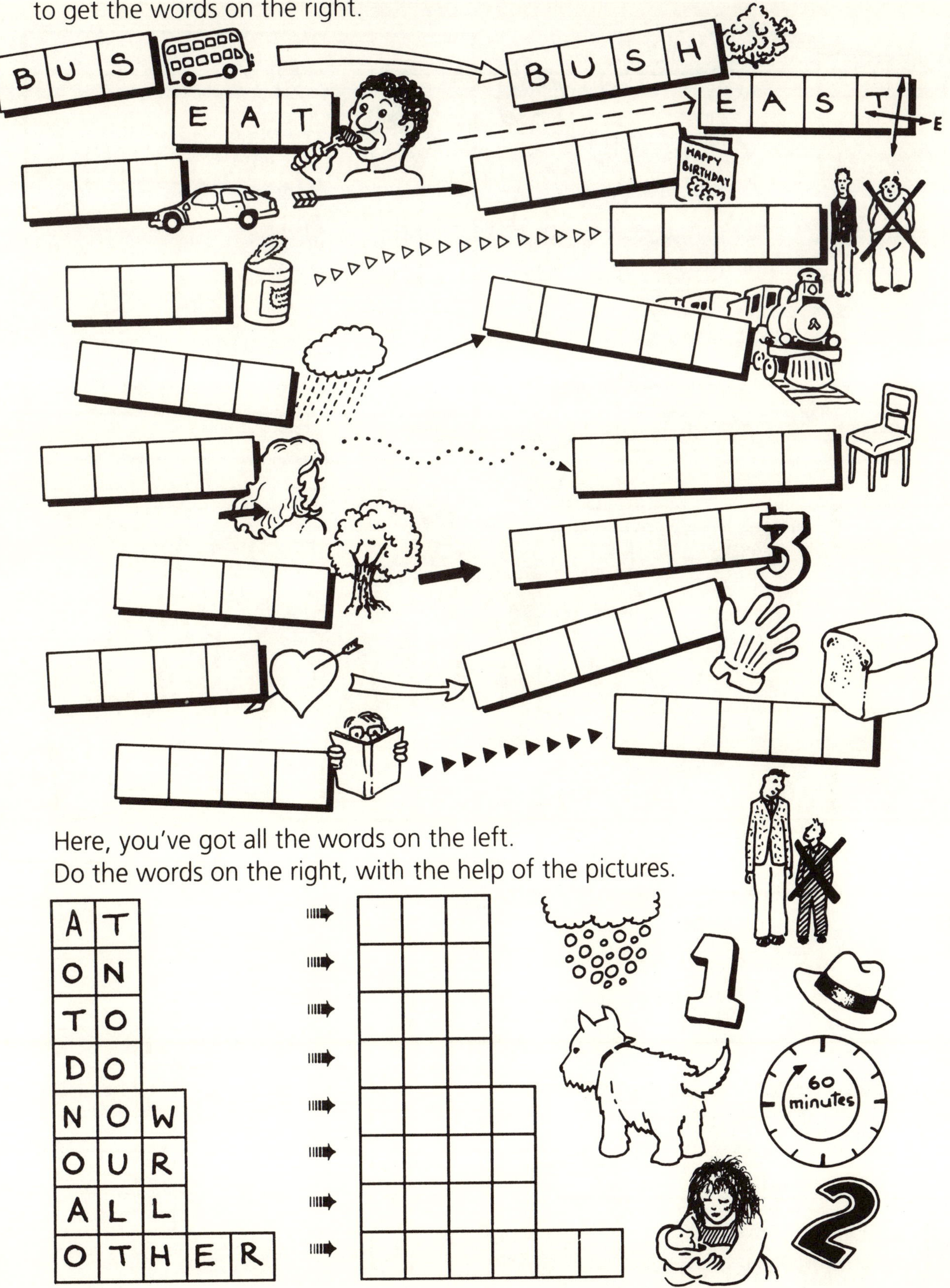
BUS
BUSH
EAT
EAST
E
HAPPY BIRTHDAY
AT
ON
TO
DO
NOW
OUR
ALL
OTHER
60 minutes

Here, you've got all the words on the left.
Do the words on the right, with the help of the pictures.

HEINEMANN ENGLISH LANGUAGE TEACHING

NAMES

Use the letters to make the names of the people.

1 LIZ
Z L L L
B I I
2 BILL
4
3
M M K O I T E
7
8
9
5
6
E B B A N A V O D D
E E P T E S U

All those names are short forms. For example, *Bill* is a short form of *William*, and *Liz* is a short form of *Elizabeth*. Put the other complete forms into the grid.
(If you have a problem, all the complete forms are in the box below.)

1 ELIZABETH
2 WILLIAM
3 4 5 6 7 8 9

Daniel David Elizabeth
Michael Peter Robert
Susan Thomas William

PHOTOCOPIABLE

THEATRE POSTERS

Put the missing words on the theatre posters. You need the words below, but on the posters you need them in their *plural* form.

BIRD	MAN	FLY
DAY	SHADOW	SON
FOX	SISTER	FROG

1
.... WITHOUT ....
by JEAN-PAUL SARTRE
2
HAPPY
....
by Samuel Beckett
M.T.W.T.F.S.S.
3
THE
....
BY Aristophanes
4
The
....
by ARISTOPHANES
5
All my
....
by Arthur Miller
6
Three
....
By Anton Chekhov
7
THE
....
BY JEAN-PAUL SARTRE
8
The Little
....
by Lillian Hellman

Do-it-yourself

All the words in this puzzle are parts of the home – six rooms and two other places. Put the letters of each word in the correct order and write the words in the grid.

LOUNGE

PHOTOCOPIABLE

At the cinema

Read the twenty film titles. (They are the titles of films from the United Kingdom and the United States.)
Ten are about a *male* person.
Ten are about a *female* person.
Write the titles in the correct grids : male or female.

QUEEN CHRISTINA US 1933
MR SMITH GOES TO WASHINGTON US 1939
THE LITTLE PRINCESS US 1939
MRS MINIVER US 1942
THE MAN FROM MOROCCO UK 1944
UNCLE SILAS UK 1947
THE BOY WITH GREEN HAIR US 1948
MY DAUGHTER JOY UK 1950
MY SON JOHN US 1952
AUNT CLARA UK 1954
GOOD MORNING, MISS DOVE US 1955
MY SISTER EILEEN US 1955
A KING IN NEW YORK UK 1957
A GIRL NAMED TAMIKO US 1962
GOODBYE, MR CHIPS UK 1969
BROTHER JOHN US 1970
THE BOYFRIEND UK 1971
THE LITTLE PRINCE US 1974
AN UNMARRIED WOMAN US 1977
THE GOOD MOTHER US 1988
QUEEN CHRISTINA

A different alphabet

The language of this town doesn't use the English alphabet. For example:

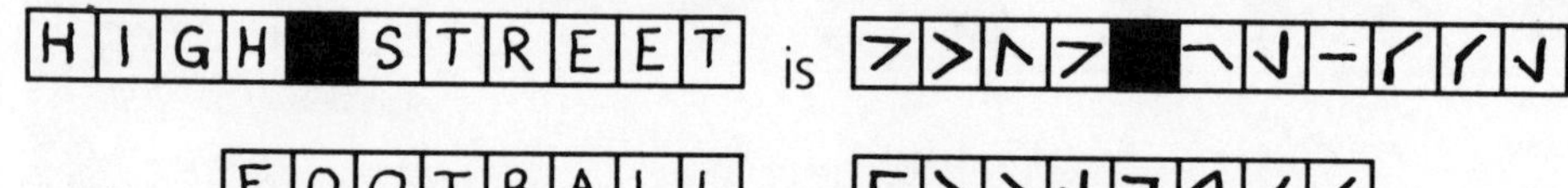
HIGH STREET
is
and
FOOTBALL
STADIUM
is

In those words you can see fifteen letters of the alphabet:

A	B	C	D	E	F	G	H	I	J	K	L	M	N	O	P	Q	R	S	T	U	V	W	X	Y	Z

Can you 'translate' the signs in the picture – and complete the alphabet grid?

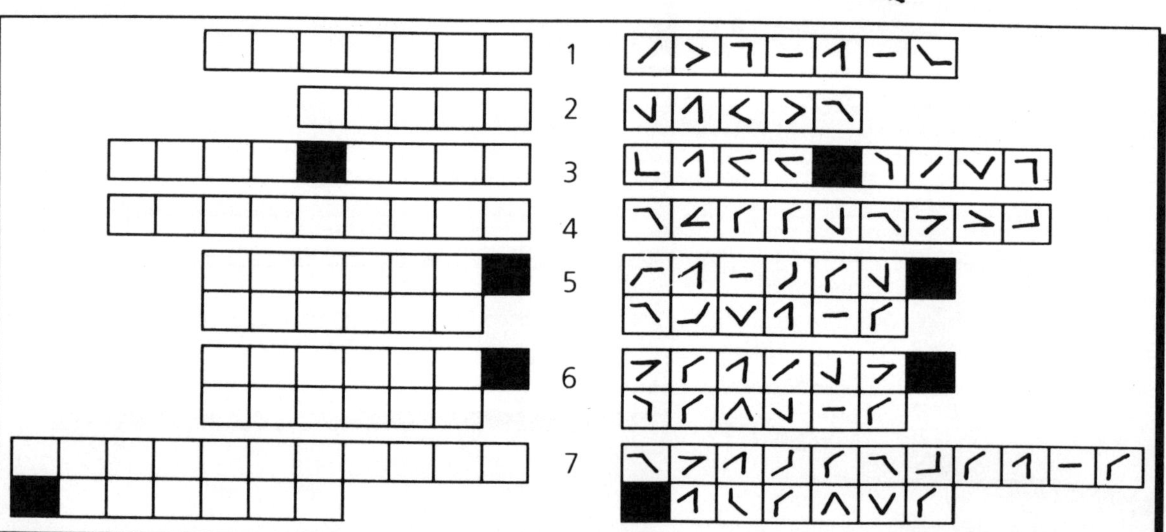
1
2
3
4
5
6
7

PHOTOCOPIABLE

Countries IN CODE

Use the code to find the names of seven more countries.

one o'clock A	two o'clock E	three o'clock I	four o'clock O	five o'clock U
ten thirty B	nine thirty C	eight thirty D	seven thirty F	six thirty G
one fifteen J	two fifteen L	three fifteen M	four fifteen N	five fifteen P
ten forty-five R	two forty-five S	six forty-five T	one forty-five Y	four forty-five Z

A Y I L T → I T A L Y

AT HOME

Write the words for the things horizontally in the grid. Then find the three English proverbs by taking the correct letters from the grid.

1 2 3 4 5 6 7 8 9 10 11 12

	a	b	c	d	e	f	g	h	i	j	k	l
1	C	O	O	K	E	R						
2												
3												
4												
5												
6												
7												
8												
9												
10												
11												
12												

Proverbs:

10b	1c	7c	9e		4f	8g		12a	6d	1e	11a	5f		4a	6d	8h		7e	11k	9b	1f	4a		5c	8g
																									.

9a	6d	2b	1f	8h	3a		12c	4i		11g	4c	9b	1a	4d		9d	5c	1d	8h		6d	12e	7c	2b
					'																			.

5f	9b	3a	9a		12f	1e	4g	9a		7e	11d	7c	2b		10d	3a		9c	8h	4g	9a
			,					,													.

PHOTOCOPIABLE

Book Titles

These books are by writers from the United Kingdom, the United States and Trinidad. Look at the pictures and put the writers' names with the titles.

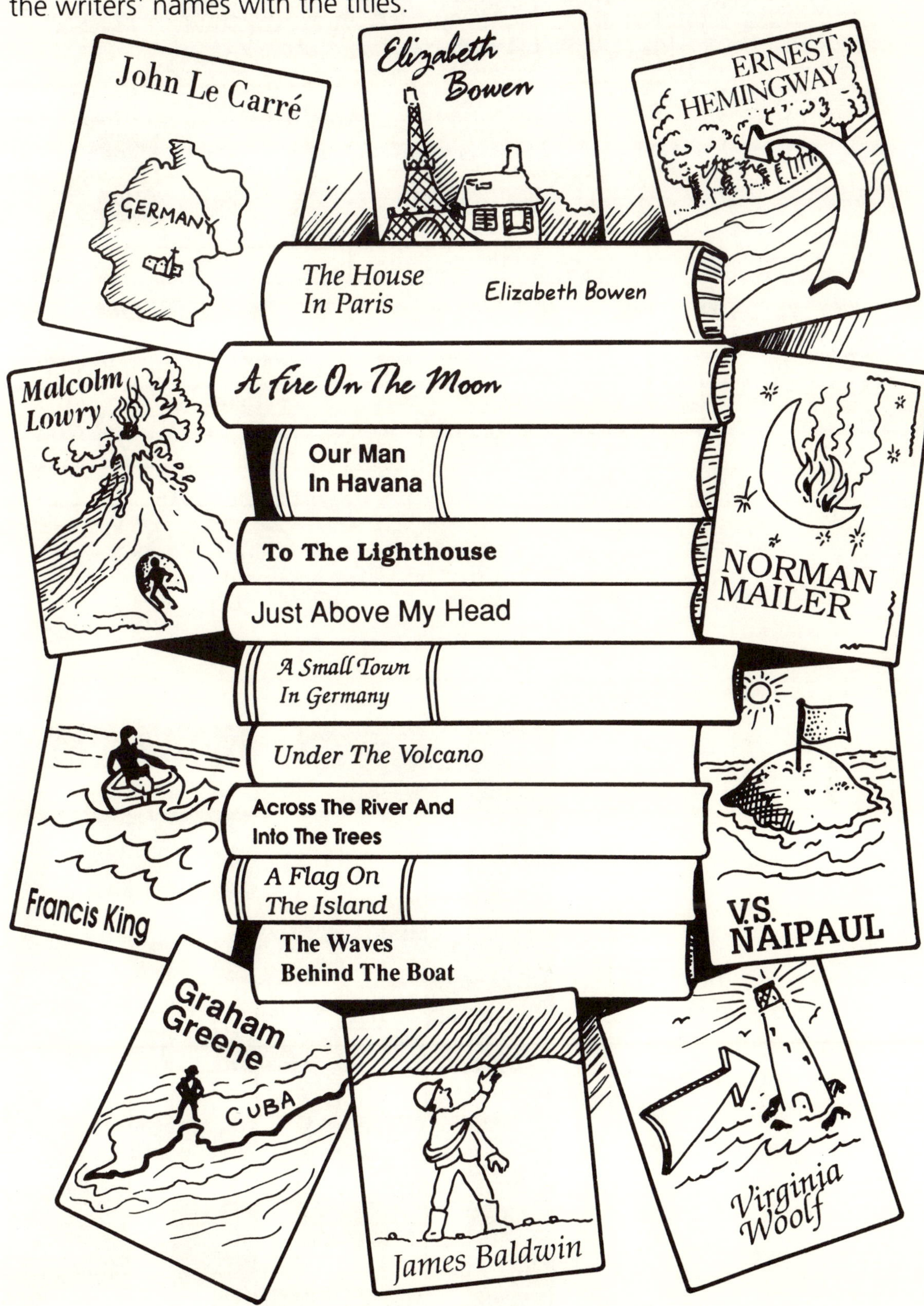
John Le Carré
GERMANY
Elizabeth Bowen
ERNEST HEMINGWAY
The House In Paris
Elizabeth Bowen
A Fire On The Moon
Malcolm Lowry
Our Man In Havana
To The Lighthouse
Just Above My Head
NORMAN MAILER
A Small Town In Germany
Under The Volcano
Across The River And Into The Trees
A Flag On The Island
The Waves Behind The Boat
Francis King
V.S. NAIPAUL
Graham Greene
CUBA
James Baldwin
Virginia Woolf

VERB CROSSWORD

Put these verbs with the correct pictures.

VERBS
ASK
BEGIN
BORROW
FINISH
PAY
PLAY
PULL
RELAX
WASH
1 BEGIN
2
3
4
5
6
7
8
9
VERBS
CARRY
EAT
GO
LISTEN
PUSH
SAY
STOP
WALK
WATCH
10 STOP
11
12
13
14
15
16
17
18

Now put the verbs into the crossword – in their *third person singular* form, like the example.
(The first group go Across; the second group go Down.)

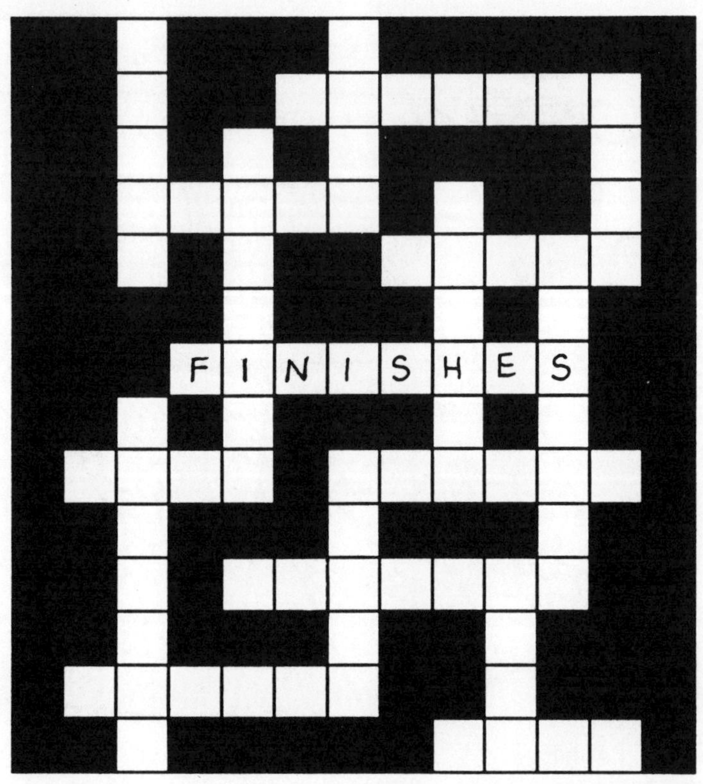
FINISHES

PHOTOCOPIABLE

Add two letters

Write the words on the left. Then add two letters to each word, to get the words on the right.

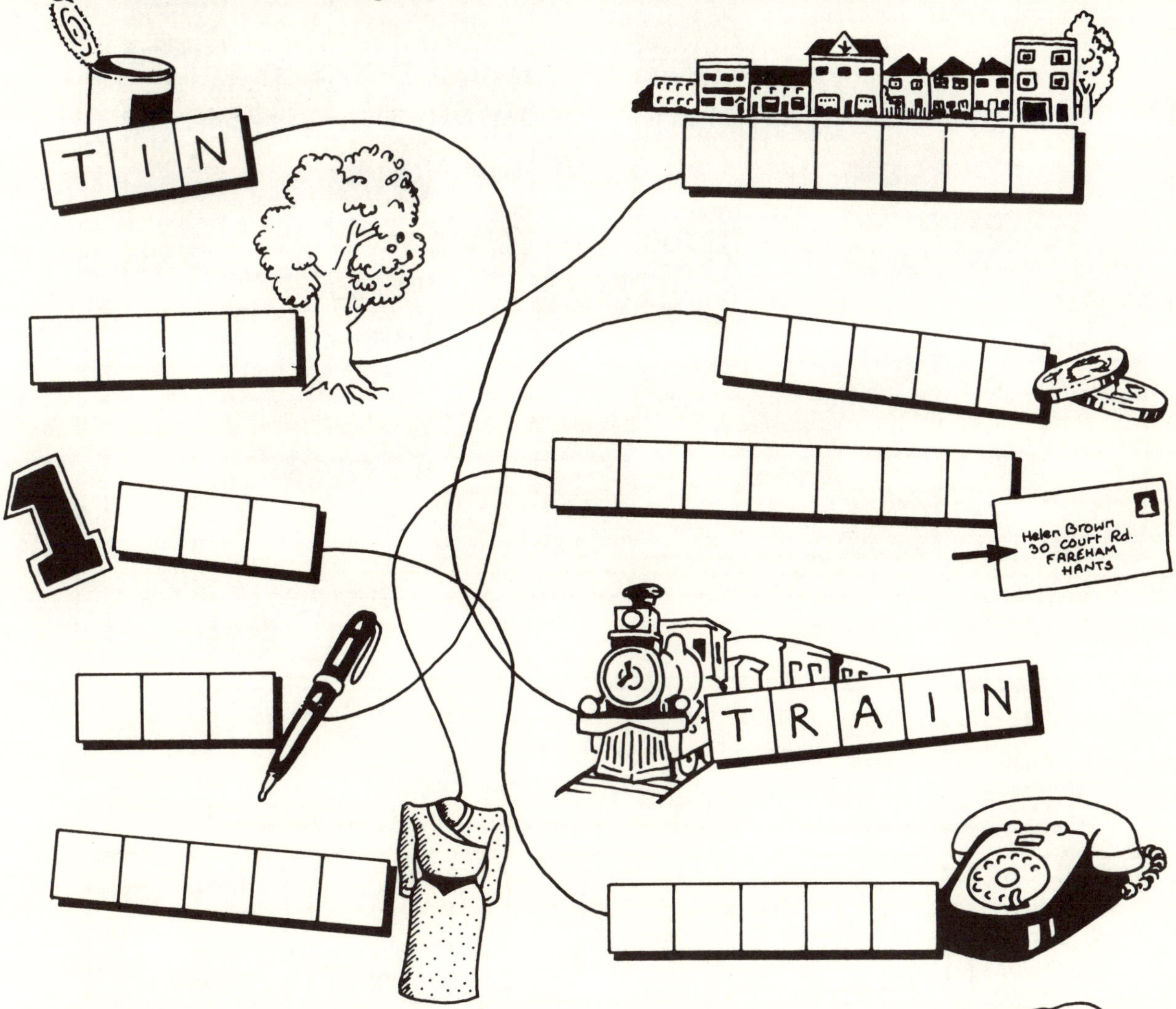

TIN

TRAIN

Helen Brown
30 Court Rd.
FAREHAM
HANTS

Here, you've got all the words on the left.
Do the words on the right, with the help of the pictures.

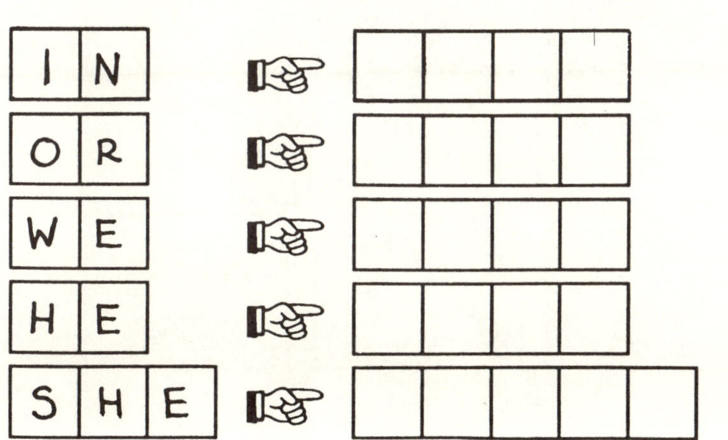

IN
OR
WE
HE
SHE

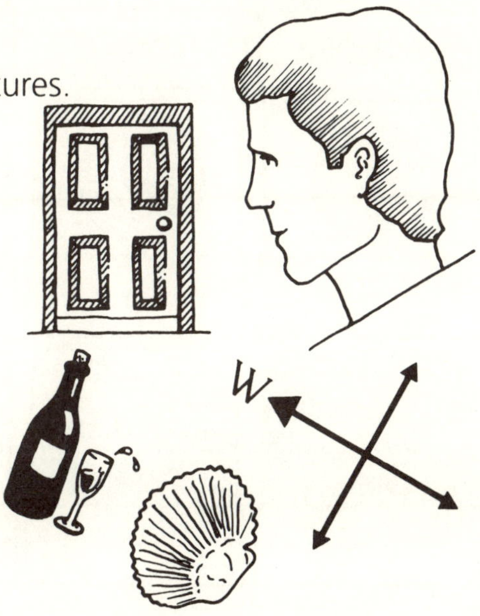

W

TV PROGRAMMES

In the crossword there are the names of fifteen programmes from British television.

						1 OUR			
					2 THE	WORLD	3 THIS	WEEK	
					ONE		WEEK		
			4 THE	SIX	O'CLOCK	NEWS		5 SIXTY	
			TRAVEL		NEWS		6 FORTY	MINUTES	
	7 THE	CLOTHES	SHOW			8 SONS			
	SKY				9 WORDS	AND	PICTURES		
10 NEWS	AT	TEN		11 QUESTION		DAUGHTERS			
	NIGHT		12 BREAK-FAST	TIME					

The crossword is complete – but look at the clues below: which clue goes with which answer?
Write the correct number and 'Across' or 'Down'.

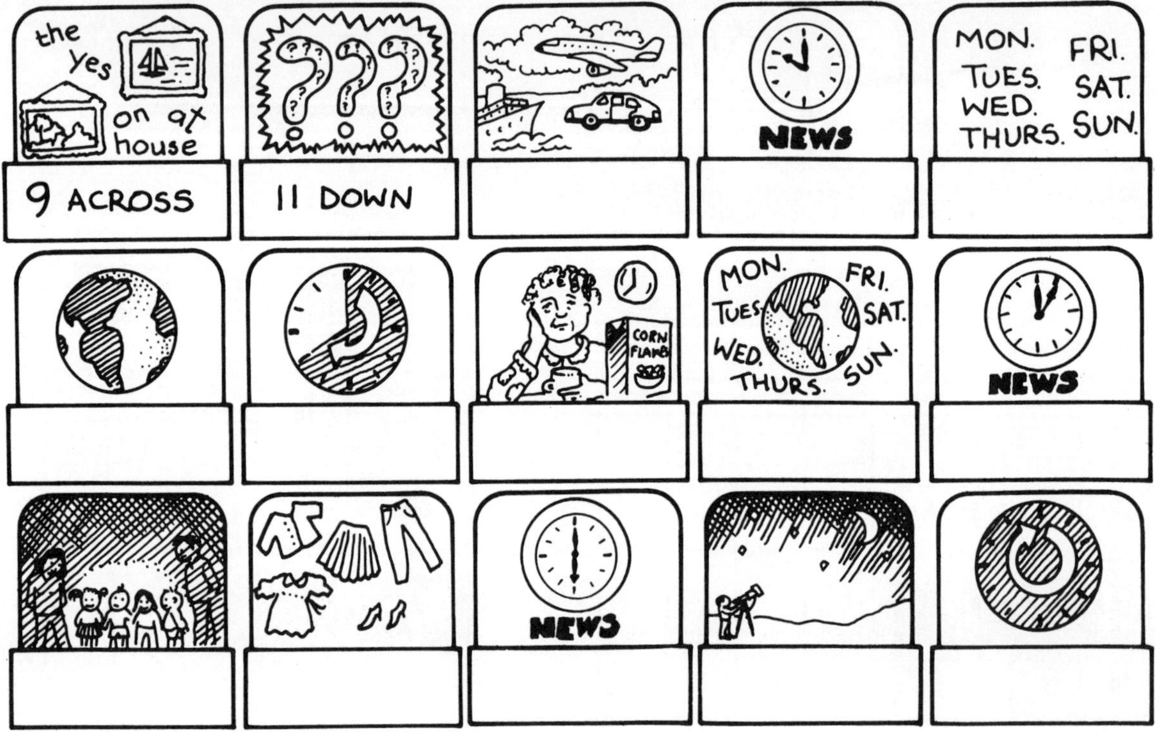

the
yes
on at
house
9 ACROSS
11 DOWN
NEWS
MON. TUES. WED. THURS. FRI. SAT. SUN.
CORN FLAKES
MON. TUES. WED. THURS. FRI. SAT. SUN.
NEWS
NEWS

PHOTOCOPIABLE

JOBS

Separate each line of letters into two jobs.
The letters for each job are in the correct order.
The pictures show one job from each pair.
Here's an example:

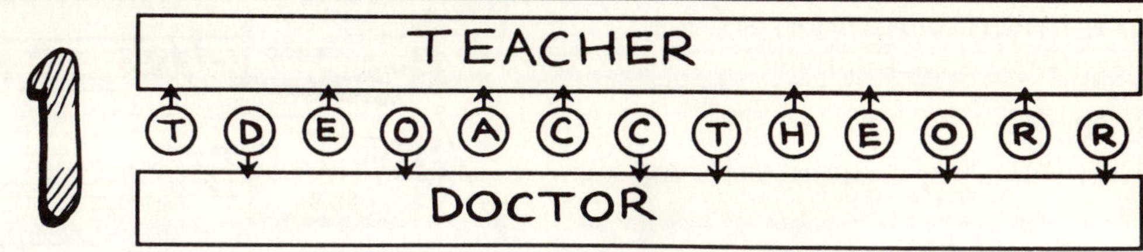
1
TEACHER
T D E O A C C T H E O R R
DOCTOR

Do these in the same way:

2
R F E P I O R R E T E M R A N

3 APIORHLIOCSETESMASN

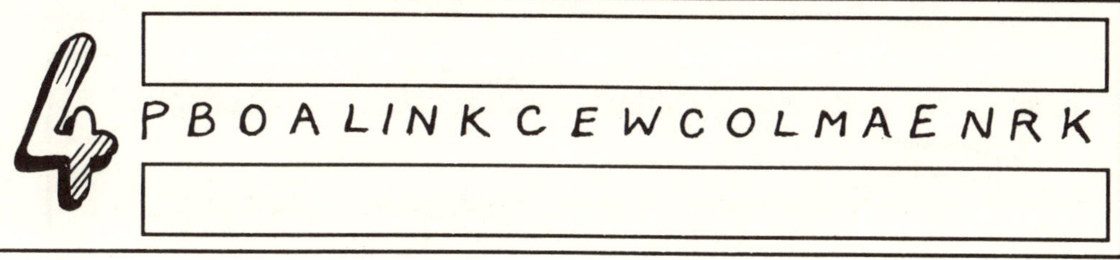
4
PBOALINKCEWCOLMAENRK

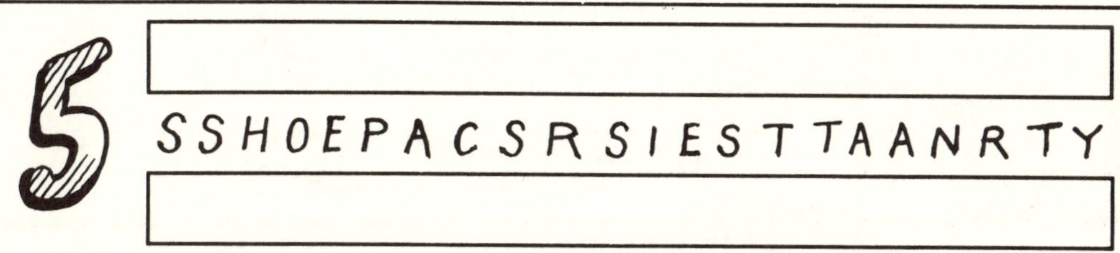
5
SSHOEPACSRSIESTTAANRTY

1
2
3
4
5
WANTED
W.P.C Robinson

Song titles

In 1963, the American group The Chiffons recorded a song called 'He's so fine'. From the title you can see that the song is about a man (*he*).

In 1964, the British group The Zombies recorded a song called 'She's not there'. From the title you can see that the song is about a woman (*she*).

THE CHIFFONS 1963	He's so fine	♂
THE ZOMBIES 1964	She's not there	♀

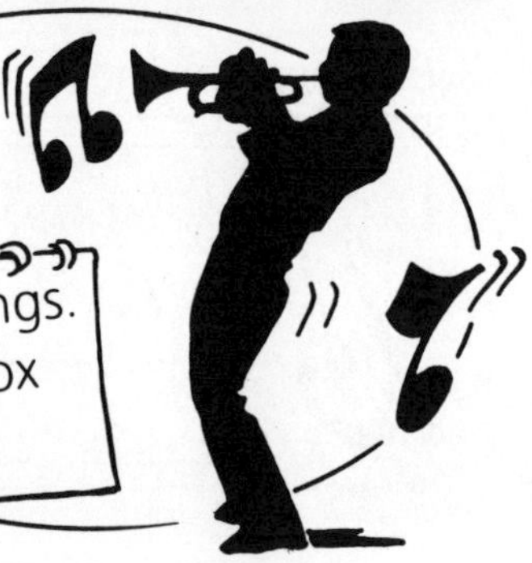

Here are ten more songs. Put ♂ or ♀ in the box after each one.

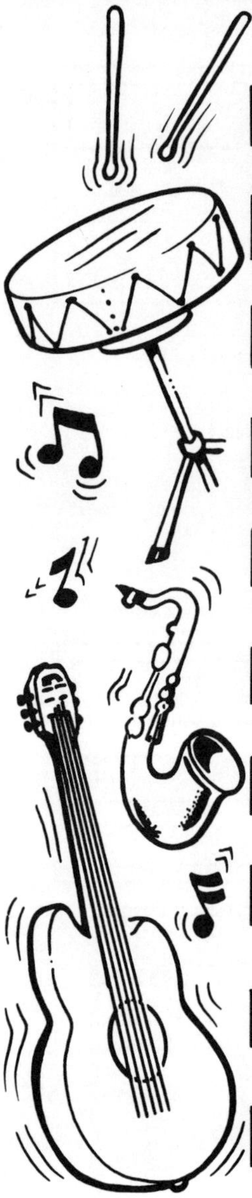

THE ROLLING STONES 1984	She was hot	☐
THE ROCKIN' BERRIES 1964	He's in town	☐
SISTER SLEDGE 1979	He's the greatest dancer	☐
DONNA SUMMER 1983	She works hard for money	☐
THE BEE GEES 1968	The singer sang his song	☐
THE WALKER BROTHERS 1965	Love her	☐
BILLY FURY 1983	Forget him	☐
RICKY VALANCE 1960	Tell Laura I love her	☐
CAMEO 1984	She's strange	☐
GANG OF FOUR 1979	At home he's a tourist	☐

PHOTOCOPIABLE

BADGES

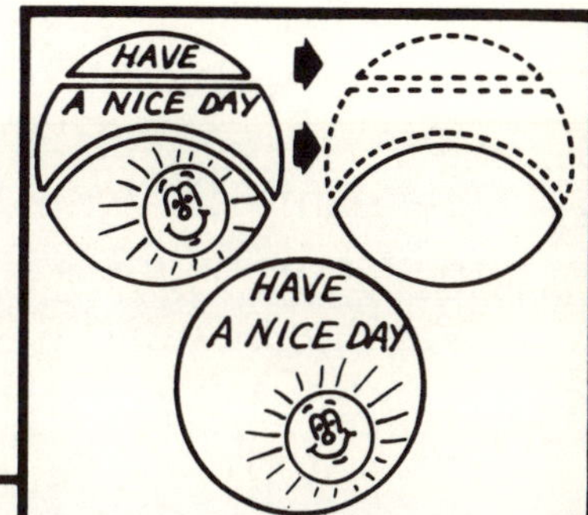

HAVE
A NICE DAY
HAVE
A NICE DAY

Assemble the badges.
For each badge, take a piece like this: 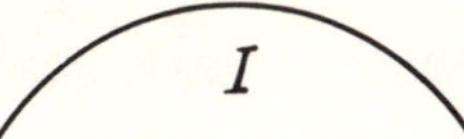
and a piece like this:  and add them to a piece like this: 

MAKE

I

DON'T READ

I AM NOT A

YES, I'M FAMOUS. DO

I'M A PERSON-

A WOMAN NEEDS A MAN LIKE

YOU RECOGNISE ME?

LOVE, NOT WAR.

A FISH NEEDS A BIKE.

THIS BADGE!

NOT A NUMBER.

TOURIST. I LIVE HERE.

LOVE NEW YORK.

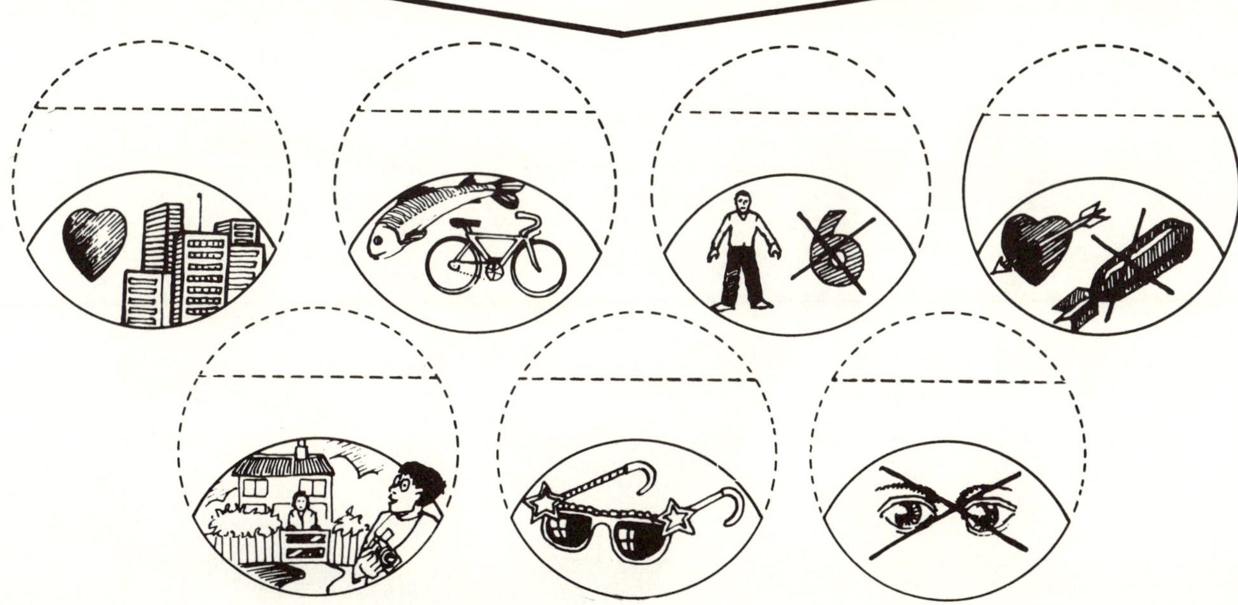

VERB BACKGAMMON

Do you know the game of 'backgammon'? This puzzle is a bit like that game: there is a board with circular pieces on it. Look at the pieces on the board. They make ten short words. Use the pieces from the box to change each short word into a verb of five letters.

For example:

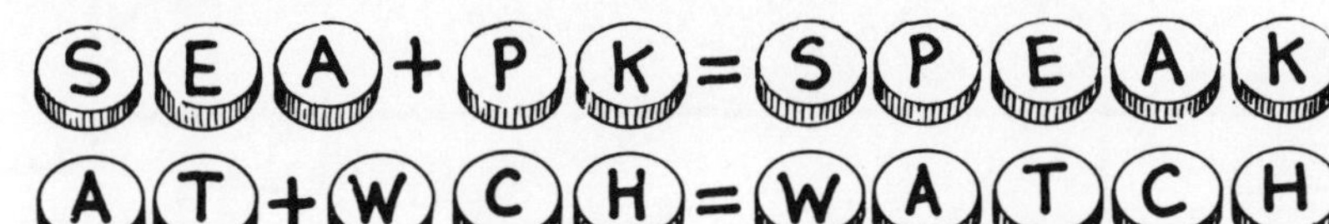

SEA + PK = SPEAK
AT + WCH = WATCH

PHOTOCOPIABLE

FRUIT

1
2
3
4
5
6
7
8
9
10

Write the words for the fruit horizontally in the grid. Then find the English proverb by taking the correct letters from the grid.

	a	b	c	d	e	f	g	h	i	j
1	K	I	W	I	F	R	U	I	T	
2										
3										
4										
5										
6										
7										
8										
9										
10										

PROVERB

7d	2e		6e	9a	9g	3a	7g		2d		6f	9e	7j		1a	5c	8b	9f	7a

10g	5b	7g		6f	3d	5a	1i	6g	7h		2b	1c	6a	5f

PHOTOCOPIABLE

Mistakes on the Signpost

There are nine spelling mistakes in the words on the signpost. Can you correct them?

ICE RINCK
BEATCH
PARCK
SNAK BAR
CHURTCH
BOOCK SHOP
BANCK
FOOTBALL MACH AT TWO O'CLOK

Pounds and pence

In the nine squares of this grid there are some British coins and notes.

one pound
fifty pence
ten pence
two pence
ten pounds
one penny
five pence
twenty pence
five pounds

Read each sum of money, and:
– write it in numbers,
– mark the correct three squares in the small grid,
like the example.

Example:

Ten pounds, three pence
£10·03p

Five pounds, eleven pence
____

Ten pounds, fifteen pence
____

Five pounds, twenty-five pence
____

Ten pounds, seventy pence
____

One pound, seven pence
____

One pound, sixty pence
____

Sixteen pounds
____

How much money is in *these* squares?

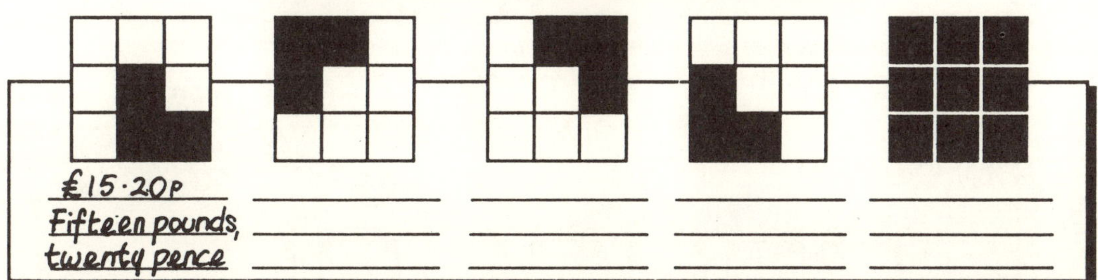
£15·20p
Fifteen pounds,
twenty pence

Musical instruments

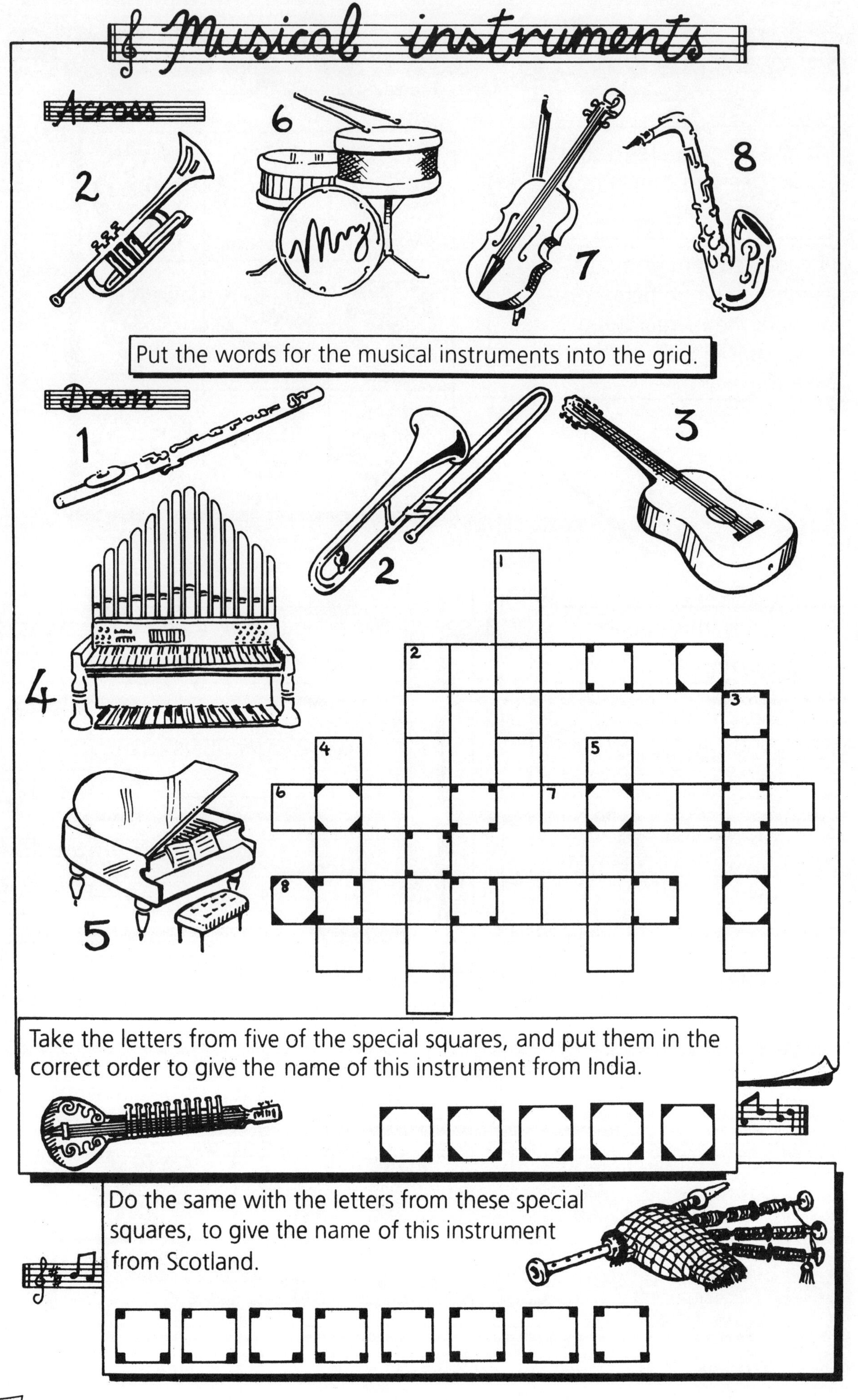

Across
2
6
7
8
Down
1
2
3
4
5

Put the words for the musical instruments into the grid.

Take the letters from five of the special squares, and put them in the correct order to give the name of this instrument from India.

Do the same with the letters from these special squares, to give the name of this instrument from Scotland.

PHOTOCOPIABLE

Write the CLUES
In this crossword, the answers are already in the squares – so write the clues!
Each clue is a verb: the Base Form of the answer.
For example: The clue for STUDYING is STUDY.
Across
1 STUDY
4
6
7
9
10
12
14
15
16
STUDYING
TELLING
DOING
SPELLING
EATING
GETTING
STARTING
RUNNING
SKATING
LEAVING
LISTENING
SWIMMING
WORKING
GOING
STOPPING
TAKING
HOPING
HELPING
OPENING
Down
2
3
5
7
8
9
11
13
15

HEINEMANN ENGLISH LANGUAGE TEACHING

RADIO PROGRAMMES

In the grid there are seventeen titles – they are all titles of BBC radio programmes.

Find them with the help of the picture-clues.

LETTER	FROM	AMERICA	THE	FOOD	PROGRAMME	THE
FARMING	SATURDAY	MONEY	BOX	JUST	A	WORLD
TODAY	NIGHT	THE	WORLD	AT	MINUTE	TONIGHT
THE	THEATRE	POETRY	BOOK-SHELF	ONE	A	BOOK
WORLD	THE	PLEASE	START	THE	WEEK	AT
THIS	SATURDAY	ROCK	SHOW	MEDICINE	THE	BEDTIME
WEEKEND	TODAY	IN	PARLIAMENT	NOW	MONDAY	PLAY

60

MON.

TONIGHT

SATURDAY

SATURDAY
SUNDAY

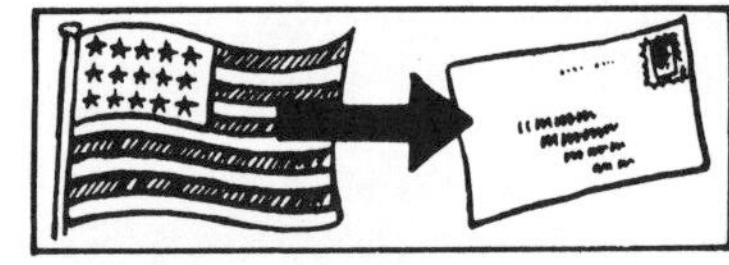

SAT.

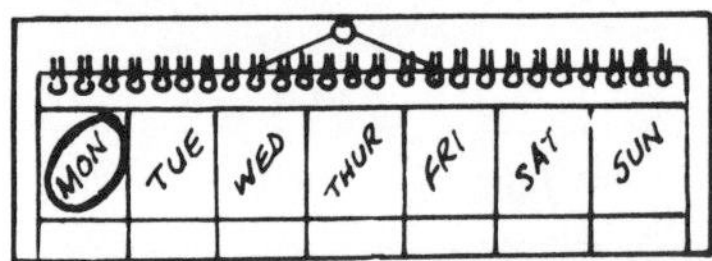
MON
TUE
WED
THUR
FRI
SAT
SUN

PHOTOCOPIABLE

FIFTEEN RECORDS

Look at the song titles on the records. Each title has 'S in it.
In some titles 'S means is.
In some titles 'S means has.
In some titles 'S is the POSSESSIVE.

Write the numbers of the songs in the correct boxes.

is	has	POSSESSIVE
		1

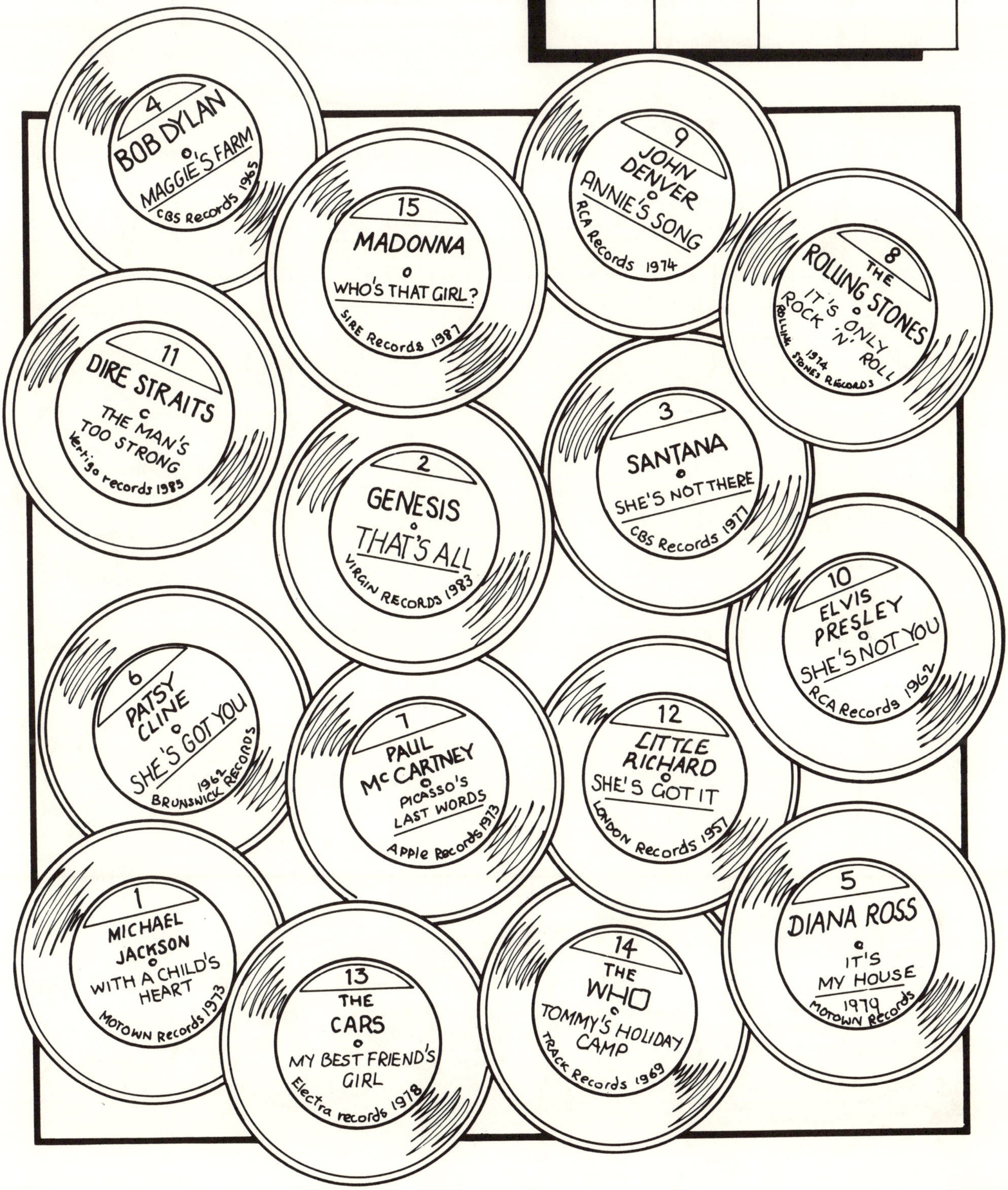

4 BOB DYLAN MAGGIE'S FARM CBS Records 1965

15 MADONNA WHO'S THAT GIRL? SIRE Records 1987

9 JOHN DENVER ANNIE'S SONG RCA Records 1974

8 THE ROLLING STONES IT'S ONLY ROCK 'N' ROLL 1974 ROLLING STONES RECORDS

11 DIRE STRAITS THE MAN'S TOO STRONG Vertigo records 1985

2 GENESIS THAT'S ALL VIRGIN RECORDS 1983

3 SANTANA SHE'S NOT THERE CBS Records 1977

10 ELVIS PRESLEY SHE'S NOT YOU RCA Records 1962

6 PATSY CLINE SHE'S GOT YOU 1962 BRUNSWICK RECORDS

7 PAUL McCARTNEY PICASSO'S LAST WORDS Apple Records 1973

12 LITTLE RICHARD SHE'S GOT IT LONDON Records 1957

1 MICHAEL JACKSON WITH A CHILD'S HEART MOTOWN Records 1973

13 THE CARS MY BEST FRIEND'S GIRL Electra records 1978

14 THE WHO TOMMY'S HOLIDAY CAMP TRACK Records 1969

5 DIANA ROSS IT'S MY HOUSE 1979 MOTOWN Records

ROUND AND ROUND

In this puzzle all the answers are words of four letters. Write the words in the correct squares, like the example.

PHOTOCOPIABLE

Letters or words?

Some English letters sound exactly like words.
For example: The letter B sounds like the word be

Complete this list:

The letter ☐ sounds like the word tea.
The letter ☐ sounds like the word queue.
The letter ☐ sounds like the word why.
The letter ☐ sounds like the word you.
The letter ☐ sounds like the word are.
The letter ☐ sounds like the word pea.
The letter ☐ sounds like the words see and sea.
The letter ☐ sounds like the words eye and I!

This looks like a list of names...

.... but it isn't! Say each name, and it sounds like a word or a phrase.
For example, ***C. Plane*** **sounds like** ***seaplane***.
Can you do the others?

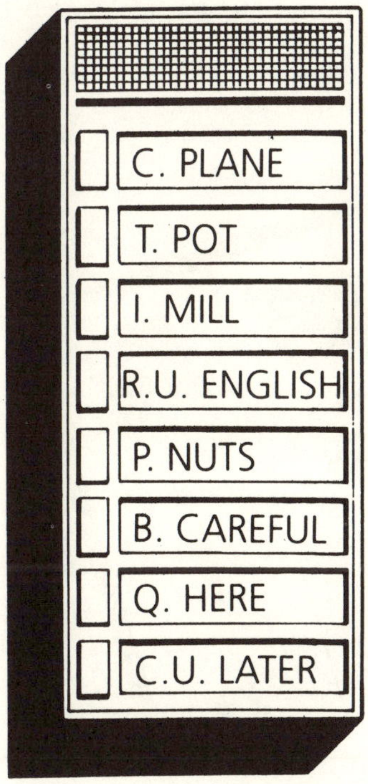

- C. PLANE
- T. POT
- I. MILL
- R.U. ENGLISH
- P. NUTS
- B. CAREFUL
- Q. HERE
- C.U. LATER

1 — —

2 — — — — — — — — ?

3 s e a p l a n e

4

5

6

7

8 — —

PHOTOCOPIABLE

DAILY NEWSPAPERS

A daily newspaper appears every *day*, and it often has the word 'daily' in its name.
Can you complete the names of these four daily newspapers from Britain?
The missing letters are all in the grid.

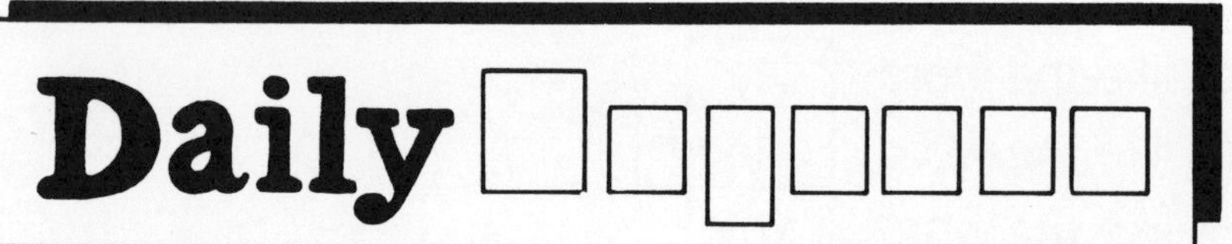
Daily

DAILY

DAILY

Daily

a s o M R
e S p r i
E r i l r
A s r m x T
DAILY

ADD THREE LETTERS

Add three letters to each word on the left, to make another word on the right. The pictures will help you.

NO → NORTH
TO
RED
PEN
FAT
ICE
OTHER
ICE
N
Do the same with these words:
US → HOUSE
IS
GO
BUT
ARE
ONE
TRUE
THEN

Rhyming pairs

The twenty-four words in the box make twelve rhyming pairs.

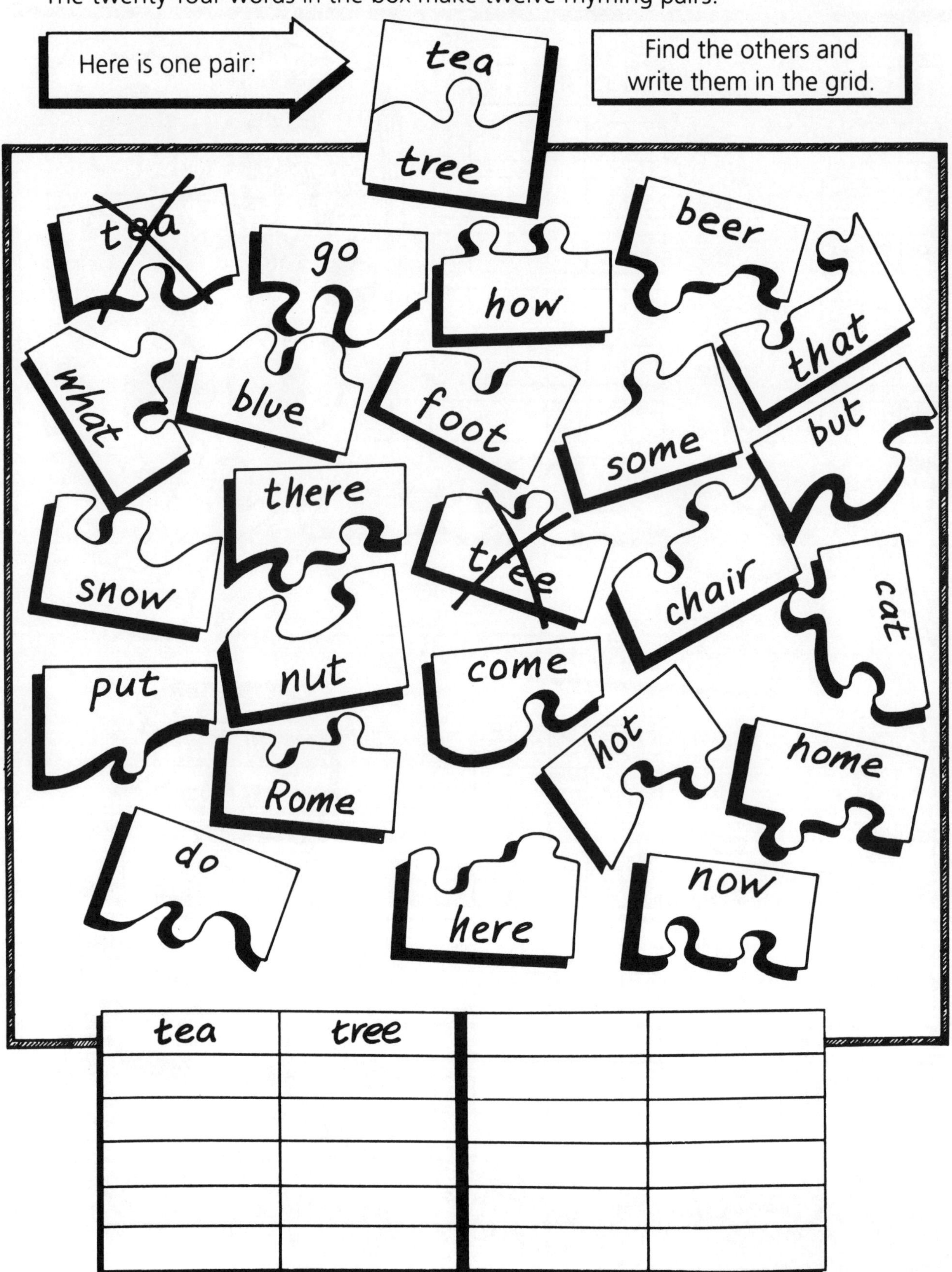

Here is one pair:
tea
tree
Find the others and write them in the grid.
tea
go
how
beer
that
what
blue
foot
some
but
there
tree
snow
chair
cat
put
nut
come
hot
home
Rome
do
here
now

tea	tree		

OLYMPIC RINGS

1
2
3
4
5
6
7
8
9
10
11
12
13
14

All the answers in this puzzle are sports – Olympic sports and others.
Put the words into the rings, in the directions shown by the flags.

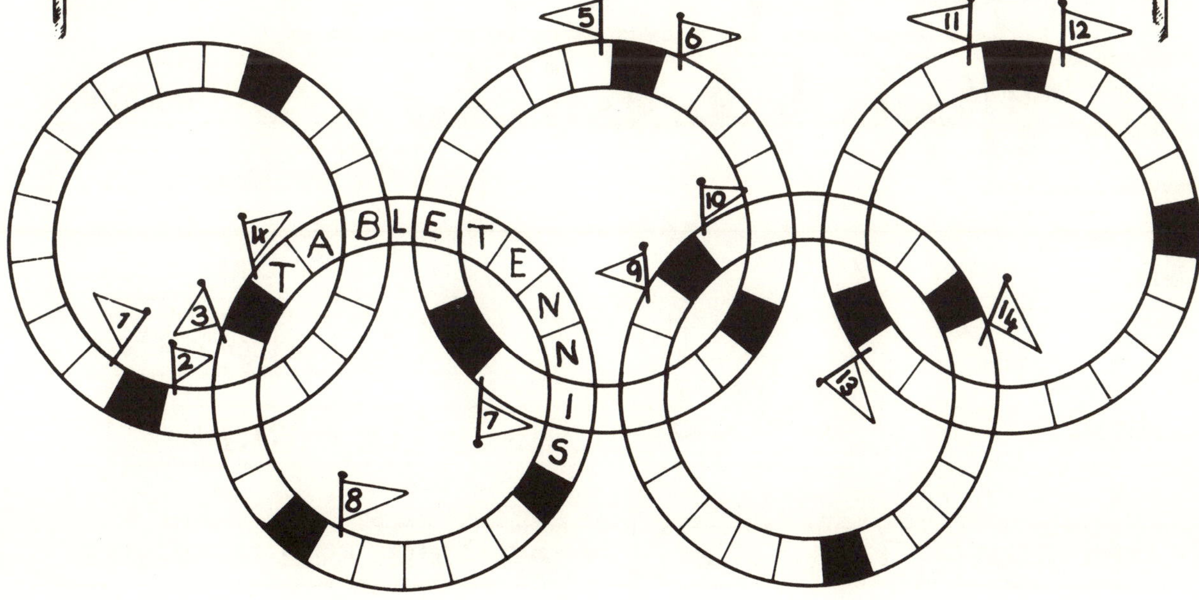

5
6
11
12
1
2
3
4
TABLETENNIS
7
8
9
10
13
14

COMPUTER KEYBOARD

This part of a piano is the *keyboard*:

Typewriters and computers also have a *keyboard* – the letters, numbers, etc. are on it.

Do you know where the letters are on an English computer keyboard? In this puzzle you can find out. Write the letters on the keyboard below.

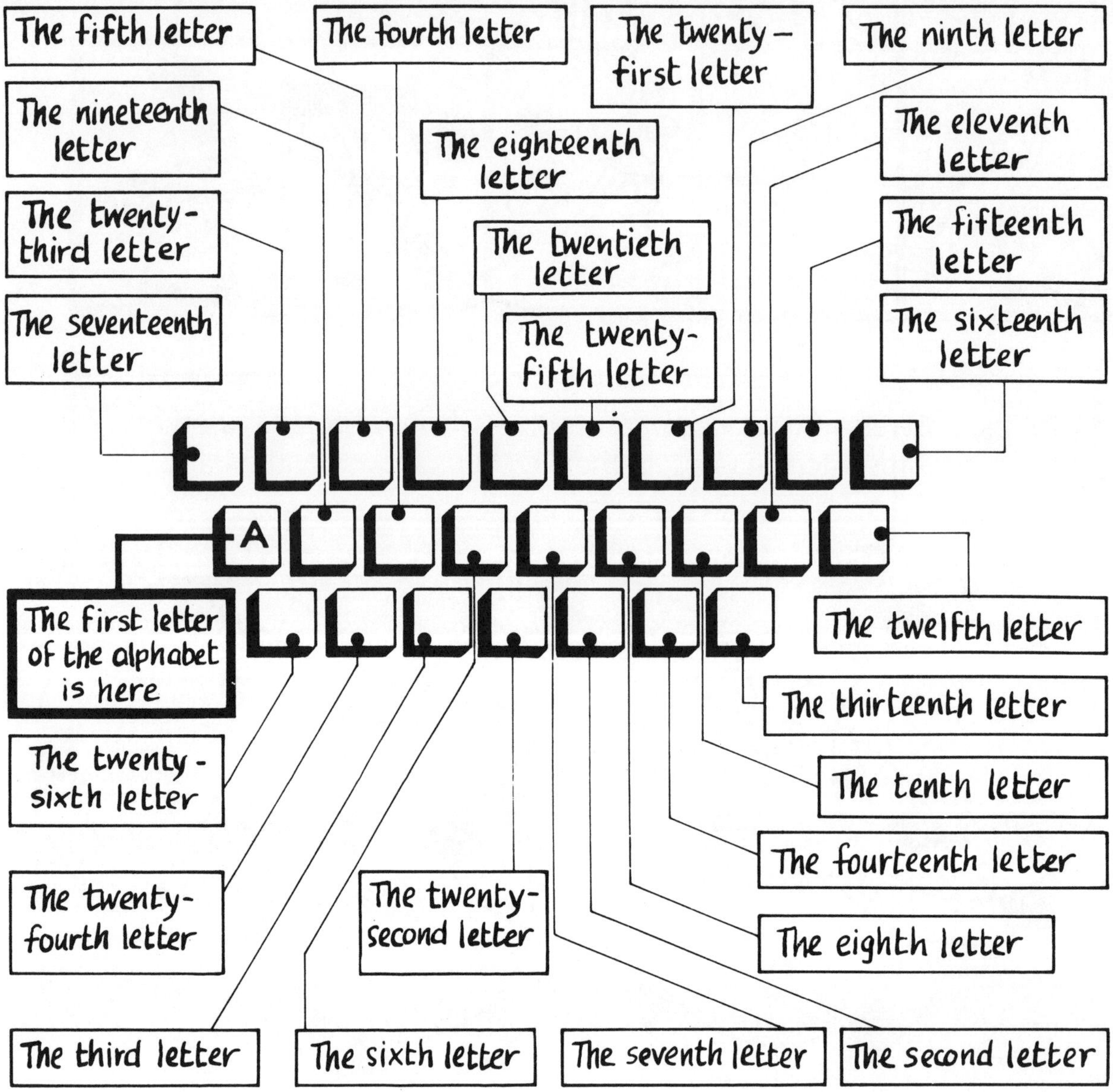

The fifth letter

The fourth letter

The twenty-first letter

The ninth letter

The nineteenth letter

The eighteenth letter

The eleventh letter

The twenty-third letter

The twentieth letter

The fifteenth letter

The seventeenth letter

The twenty-fifth letter

The sixteenth letter

A

The first letter of the alphabet is here

The twelfth letter

The thirteenth letter

The twenty-sixth letter

The tenth letter

The fourteenth letter

The twenty-fourth letter

The twenty-second letter

The eighth letter

The third letter

The sixth letter

The seventh letter

The second letter

PHOTOCOPIABLE

ANIMALS

The English words for ten animals are in the grid – broken into parts. Find the correct parts and assemble them.

tor	ca	rot	al	rab
on	li	cha	on	der
mel	ga	toise	le	ra
cob	me	ga	tor	par
spi	kan	li	bit	roo

1
lion
2

3
4
5
6

7
8
9
10

PHOTOCOPIABLE

SHAPES AND LETTERS

Do you know these English words?

square triangle circle

Those words are in this puzzle.

Use the letters in the shapes to make the six words in the boxes. Then answer the question at the bottom of the page.

N
S
A
T
E
U
P

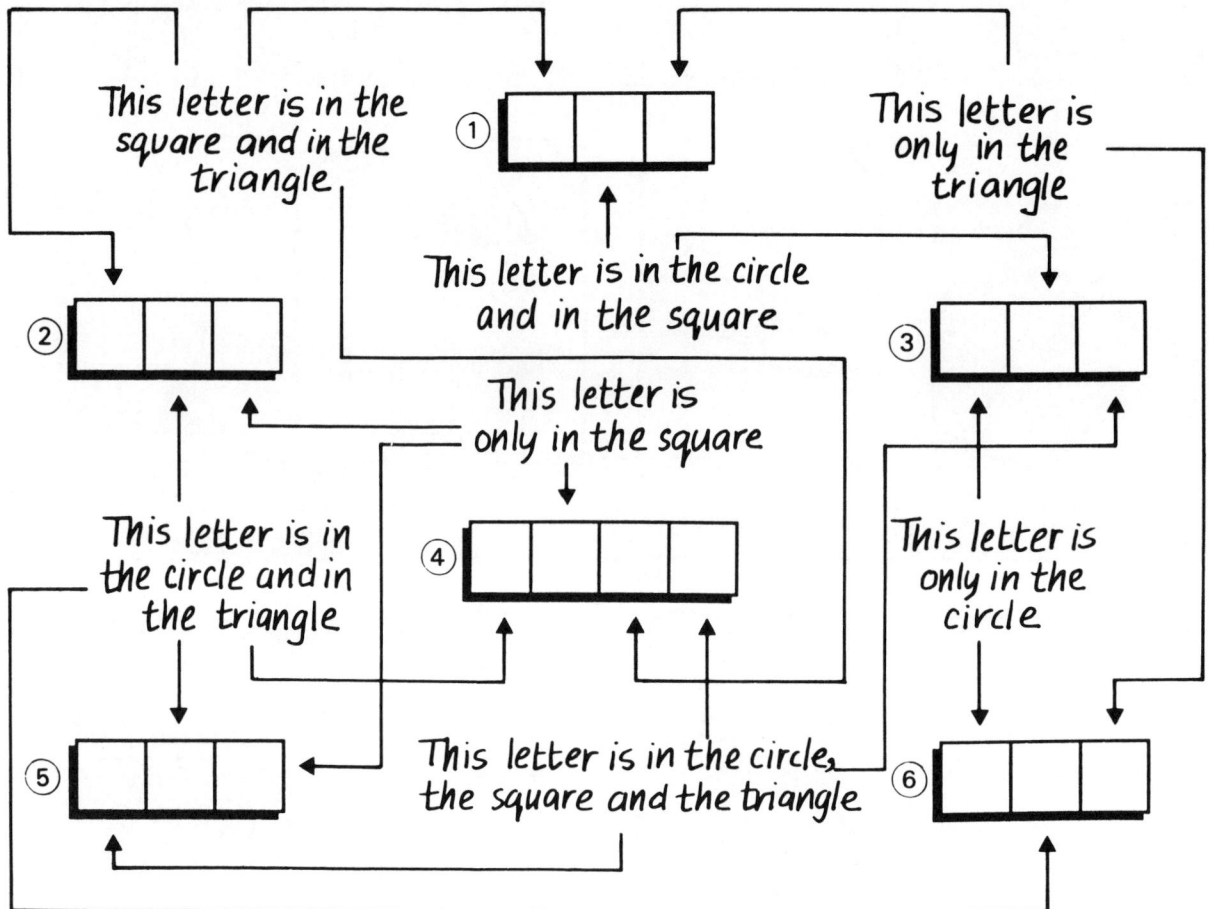

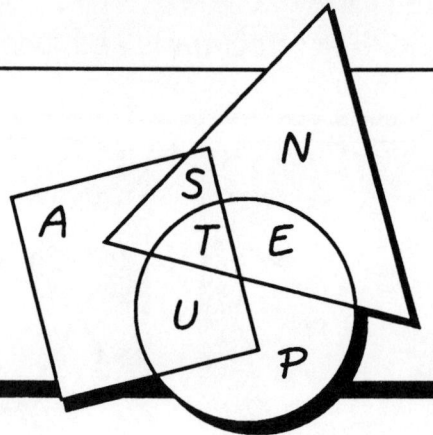

This letter is in the square and in the triangle

① □□□

This letter is only in the triangle

This letter is in the circle and in the square

② □□□

③ □□□

This letter is only in the square

④ □□□□

This letter is in the circle and in the triangle

This letter is only in the circle

⑤ □□□

This letter is in the circle, the square and the triangle

⑥ □□□

Question: Can you make an English word with all seven letters from the shapes?

□□□□□□□

PHOTOCOPIABLE

MORE NEWSPAPERS

In this puzzle, there are the names of six British newspapers.
Can you assemble the names from the pieces in the grid?
Here's a little help: five of the names begin with the word *the*, and one doesn't.

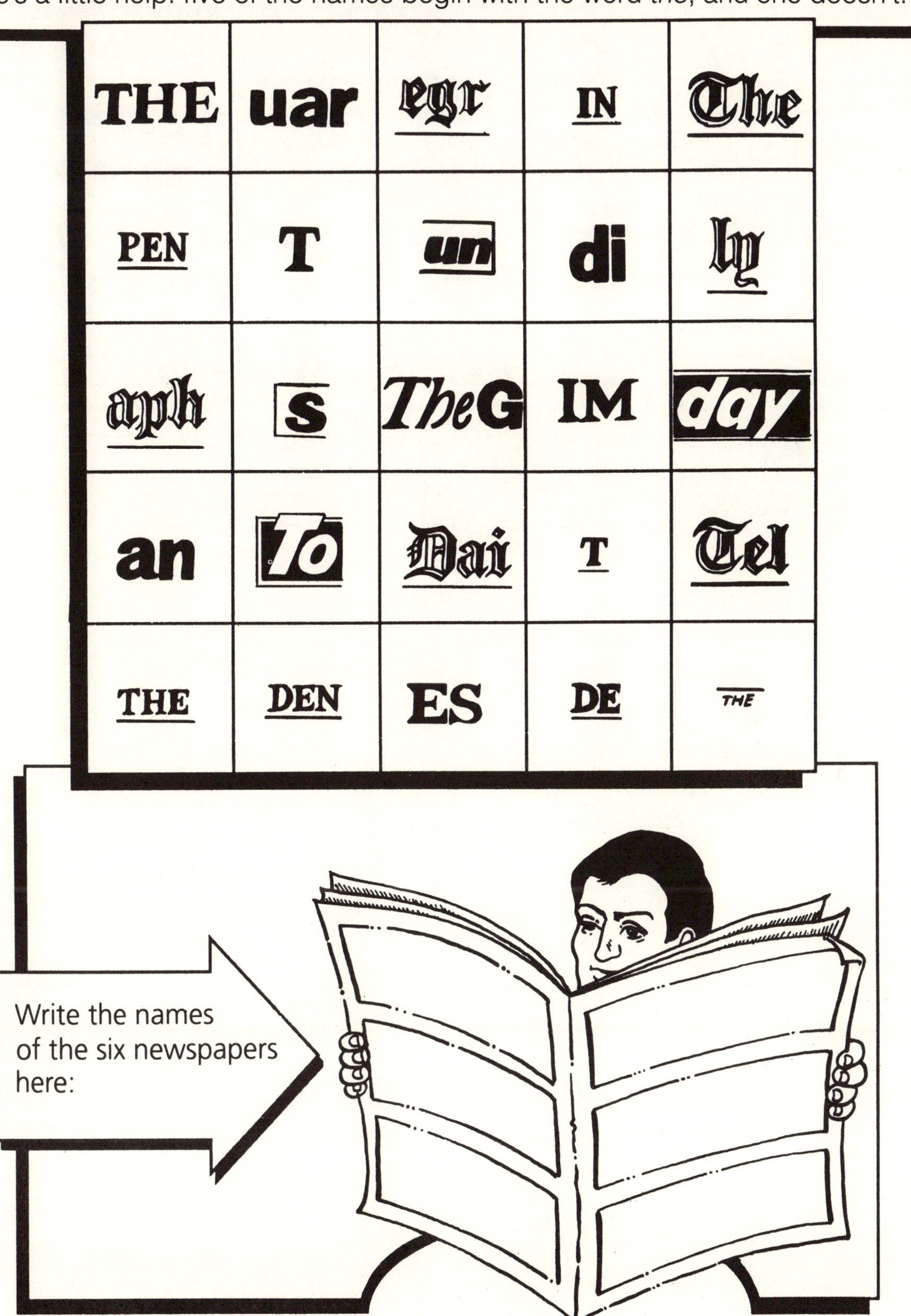

THE
uar
egr
IN
The
PEN
T
un
di
ly
aph
s
TheG
IM
day
an
To
Dai
T
Tel
THE
DEN
ES
DE
THE
Write the names of the six newspapers here:

RADIO STATIONS

Here are seven radio stations. You can hear them all in London.

G.L.R.
GREATER LONDON RADIO
94·9 MHZ
BBC
Radio
3
92·5
MHZ
BBC
Radio 1
88 MHZ
91 MHZ
BBC
RADIO
2
BBC
Radio 4
95 MHZ
LBC
97·3 MHZ
CAPITAL
RADIO
95·8 MHZ

Write the correct radio station for each speaker.

1
THIS IS
....
ON NINETY-ONE
MEGAHERTZ.

2
THIS IS
....
ON NINETY-FIVE
MEGAHERTZ.

3
THIS IS
....
ON NINETY-SEVEN
POINT THREE
MEGAHERTZ.

4
THIS IS
....
ON NINETY-TWO
POINT FIVE
MEGAHERTZ.

5
THIS IS
....
ON NINETY-FIVE
POINT EIGHT
MEGAHERTZ.

6
THIS IS
....
ON EIGHTY-EIGHT
MEGAHERTZ.

7
THIS IS
....
ON NINETY-FOUR
POINT NINE
MEGAHERTZ.

PAST AND PRESENT

You can make the *Past Simple* of a lot of English verbs by just changing one letter.

For example:

SING
SANG
DRIVE
DROVE

Do the same with the twelve verbs in the puzzle.

Here are the twelve letters you need.

A A A A A A A E E O O O

C	O	M	E

R	U	N

D	R	I	N	K

F	A	L	L

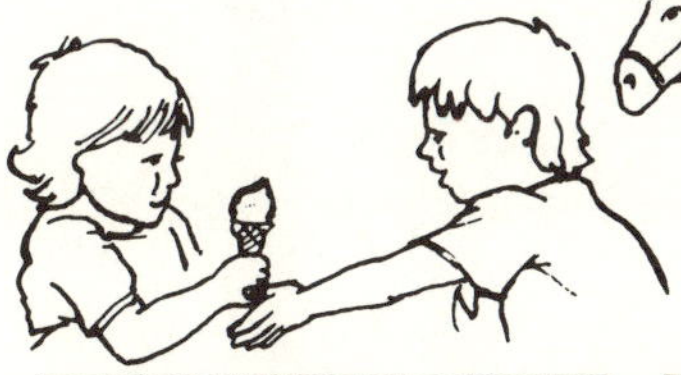

G	I	V	E

R	I	D	E

R	I	N	G

S	W	I	M

W	I	N

T	H	R	O	W

W	R	I	T	E

S	I	T

Books BOOKS Books

In each group of four books, put the same two letters in the squares to complete the titles. For example, in the first group you need the letters AR.

- H[AR]D TIMES — Charles Dickens
- KANG[AR]OO — D.H. Lawrence
- ANIMAL F[AR]M — George Orwell
- THE YE[AR]S — Virginia Woolf

- A ROOM WI[ ] A VIEW — E.M. Forster
- [ ]EY CAME TO A CITY — J.B. Priestley
- TWELF[ ] NIGHT — William Shakespeare
- O[ ]ELLO — William Shakespeare

- LEFT H[ ]D, RIGHT H[ ]D — Osbert Sitwell
- M[ ] [ ]D SUPERM[ ] — George Bernard Shaw
- ROMEO [ ]D JULIET — William Shakespeare
- NIGHT [ ]D DAY — Virginia Woolf

- M[ ] AND WOM[ ] — Robert Browning
- THE SEV[ ] SEAS — Rudyard Kipling
- THE SECRET AG[ ]T — Joseph Conrad
- NINETE[ ] EIGHTY-FOUR — George Orwell

- GOODBYE TO BERL[ ] — Christopher Isherwood
- THE TIME MACH[ ]E — H.G. Wells
- STRANGE MEET[ ]G — Susan Hill
- ROB[ ]SON CRUSOE — Daniel Defoe

Now you can complete eight more titles. Look very carefully at the corners of the squares!

- [ ]E GRE[ ] M[ ] — Kingsley Amis
- [ ]E [ ]IRD M[ ] — Graham Greene
- [ ]E G[ ]D[ ] P[ ]TY — Katherine Mansfield
- MR NORRIS CH[ ]GES TRA[ ]S — Christopher Isherwood
- [ ]E OLD M[ ] AT [ ]E ZOO — Angus Wilson
- [ ]E ISL[ ]D — Aldous Huxley
- [ ]E [ ]VISIBLE M[ ] — H.G. Wells
- [ ]E W[ ] OF [ ]E WORLDS — H.G. Wells

PHOTOCOPIABLE

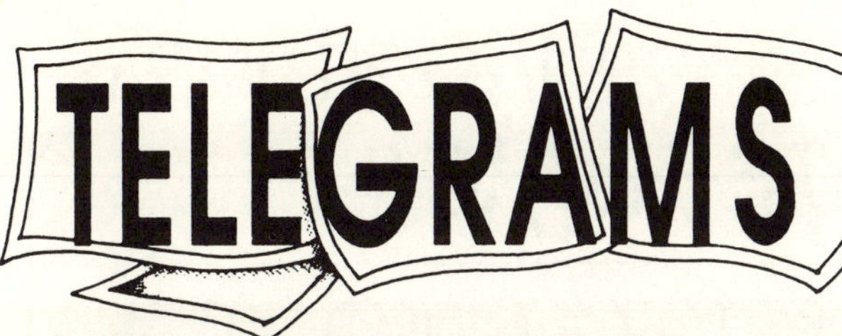
TELEGRAMS

TELEGRAMS
TELEGRAMS
LBL 12

These telegrams have mistakes in them: the numbers 1-8 appear instead of some letters, e.g. 6=A.

1 2 3 4 5 6 7 8
A

Which letters do the other numbers represent? And what do the telegrams say?

1

Telegram one
86PP7 C8R532M63!

2

Telegram two
86PP7 N1W 716R !

3

Telegram three
86PP7 B5R28D67!

4

Telegram four

86PP7
2W1N27 - F5R32
B5R28D67!

5

Telegram five

W1LL D4N1! 74U
P6331D 74UR DR5V5NG
2132!

6

Telegram six

C4NGR62UL6254N3!
74U P6331D 74UR
1X6M!

Mixed Vegetables

A E
M O
O S
T T
C E E N O R S
T
W
B
C
C
E
M R
U
U
A E O O
P S T T
H
M M O O
R S S U
I N
N O O
S
A E
P S
C E
E G
O R
S T T
U
A
C O R R S T
E
E
E E E
E
E
E

Put the letters of each word in the correct order. Then put the words in the correct places in the crossword.

VERB DICE

On these dice, there are the letters of two verbs in the *Past Simple* tense:

S
K
P
E
W P A
T
L
D
D
O
E
WALKED
STOPPED

Find the verbs on the other dice and write them in the boxes.

1 ☐☐☐☐☐☐☐

2 ☐☐☐☐☐☐

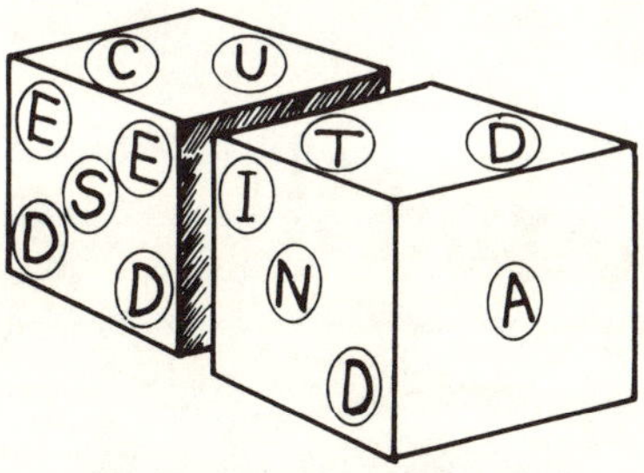

3 ☐☐☐☐☐☐

4 ☐☐☐☐☐☐

5 ☐☐☐☐☐

6 ☐☐☐☐☐☐☐

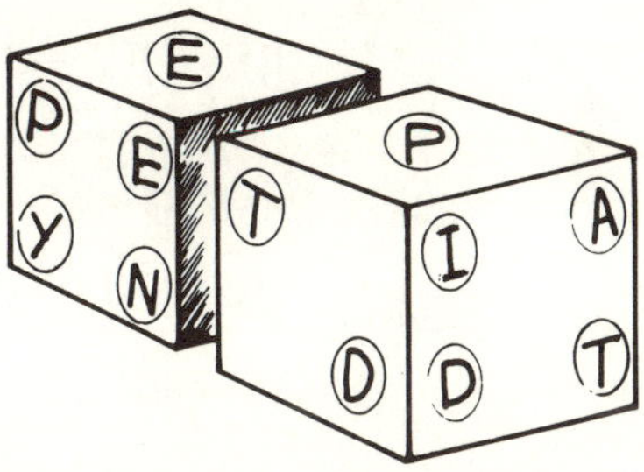

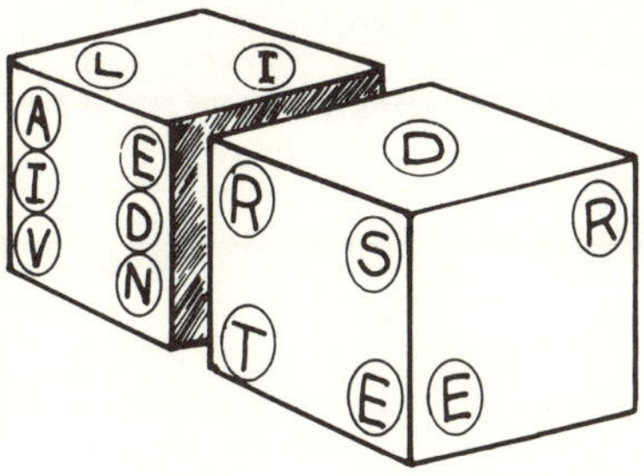

7 ☐☐☐☐☐☐☐

8 ☐☐☐☐☐☐☐☐

9 ☐☐☐☐☐☐

10 ☐☐☐☐☐☐

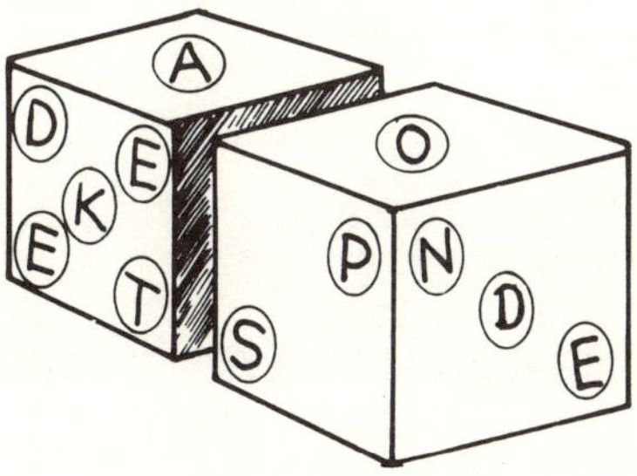

RECORD STORE

In the song titles, each symbol represents a word. The words are: HOW, WHAT, WHERE, WHO, WHY, AM, IS and ARE. Work out which word each symbol represents, and write the complete titles.

1. ◆ ◇ LOVE? — Howard Jones
2. ▲ CAN'T WE LIVE TOGETHER? — Sade
3. ▼ WEARS THESE SHOES? — Elton John
4. ■ DID YOUR HEART GO? — WHAM!
5. ◆ CAN I SAY? — Boz Scaggs
6. ● CAN I BE SURE? — Dusty Springfield
7. ▼ △ I? — Adam Faith
8. ▲ DON'T THEY UNDERSTAND? — George Hamilton
9. ◆ ◇ A MAN? — The Four Tops
10. ■ DO WE GO FROM HERE? — Cliff Richard
11. ▼ ◇ IT? — Mantronix
12. ● CAN YOU MEND A BROKEN HEART? — The Bee Gees
13. ■ ▽ YOU NOW? — Jackie Trent
14. ▼ ▽ YOU? — The ▼

●	=	▲	=	▼	=	◇	= ....
■	=	◆	=	△	=	▽	= ....

1		8	
2		9	
3		10	
4		11	
5		12	
6		13	
7		14	

PHOTOCOPIABLE

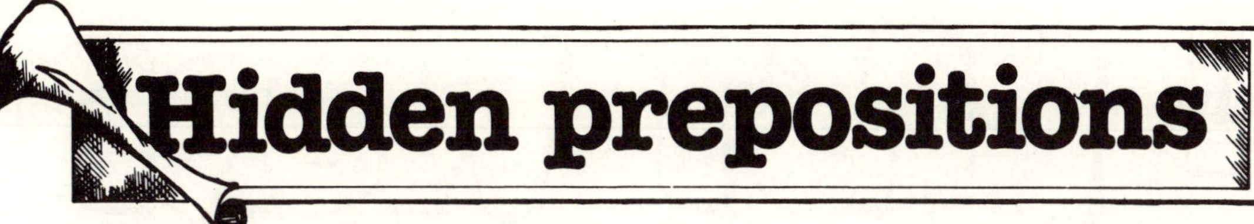

Hidden prepositions

Look at these two sentences:

IT'S EIGHT O'CLOCK.

I LIKE THE STREETS OF ROME.

In each sentence, there is a 'hidden' preposition, using letters from more than one word:

IT'S EIGHT O'CLOCK.
TO
I LIKE THE STREETS OF ROME.
FROM

Can you find the 'hidden' prepositions in these sentences?
Like *to* and *from* ,they are all prepositions of place.
Draw a box round each one.

1
WE DIDN'T GO NORTH, WE WENT SOUTH.
2
SUSAN AND JANE ARE SISTERS.
3
WE BOUGHT A NEW SOFA THIS AFTERNOON.
4
THIS WINDOW NEEDS SOME OIL.
5
LET'S VISIT MIAMI NEXT YEAR.
MIAMI
6
IN TIBET WE ENDED OUR JOURNEY.
TIBET
7
CAN I BORROW A POUND, ERNEST?
8
DID IT RAIN TODAY?

Write the eight prepositions here in **alphabetical** order.

□□	□□□□
□□□□□□□	□□□□
□□□□	□□
□□	□□□□□

THE LAST WORD

Each of these contractions is the last word in two sentences.
Put them in the correct places.

aren't. | can't. | weren't. | didn't. | isn't. | don't. | doesn't. | haven't. | hasn't. | wasn't.

Read the sentences on the left like this: → ← And the sentences on the right like this:

The U.S.A. is a big country, but England	1 isn't.	The Colosseum is in Rome, but the Eiffel Tower
The library is open, but the shops	2	Bob and Jack are good friends, but Tom and Jerry
Shakespeare was English, but Galileo	3	The match was good, but the weather
The Wright brothers were American, but the Brontë sisters	4	I was at home yesterday, but my mother and father
My friends went to the concert, but I	5	Shakespeare wrote plays, but Picasso
My sister likes jazz, but I	6	Fish live in water, but lions
Anne goes to school by bike, but Sue	7	I like reading, but my sister
My friend has got a computer, but I	8	Mr and Mrs Jones have got two cars, but we
I have got a bike, but my brother	9	My mother has got a job, but my father
Birds can fly, but elephants	10	My sister can play the piano, but I

PHOTOCOPIABLE

PICTURES AND OPPOSITES

Each answer in this crossword has five letters. Some clues are pictures. Other clues are words: for these, write the *opposite* word in the grid.

BREAD
HEAVY
ACROSS
Picture clues
DOWN

Opposite clues

	ACROSS
12	light
14	thin
17	asleep
24	late

DOWN			
2	clean	16	true
3	expensive	17	accompanied
4	long	18	full
5	left	19	right
15	north	20	dark

HEINEMANN ENGLISH LANGUAGE TEACHING

Months jigsaw

Look at this piece from the jigsaw:
All the letters of the alphabet are on it, except A,G,S,T and U. With those letters you can make a month: AUGUST.
Find the other months and write them in the correct places on the assembled jigsaw.

F	R	O	D	J
Q	B	I	V	Y
H	L	E	Z	
M	X	N	P	
W	C	K		

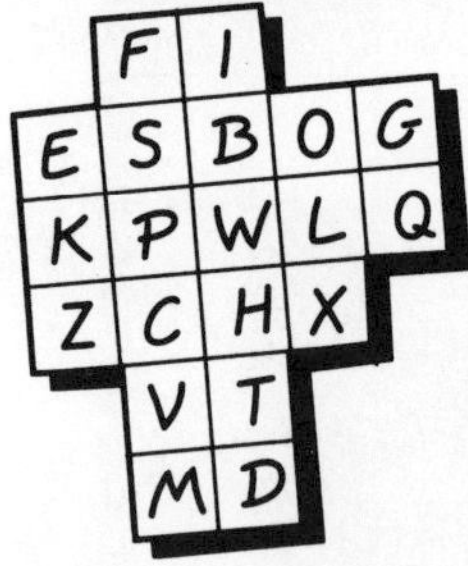
F I
E S B O G
K P W L Q
Z C H X
V T
M D

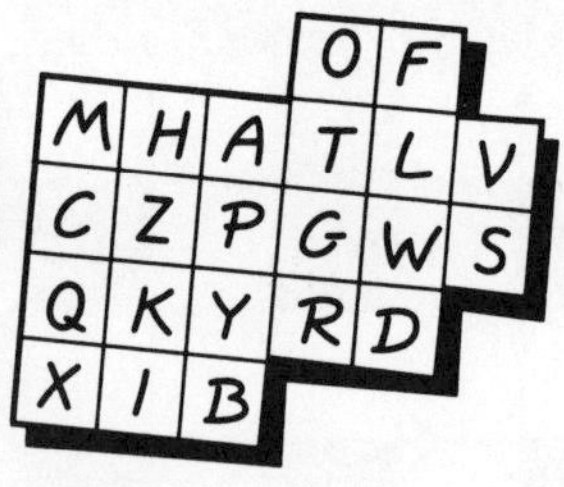
O F
M H A T L V
C Z P G W S
Q K Y R D
X I B

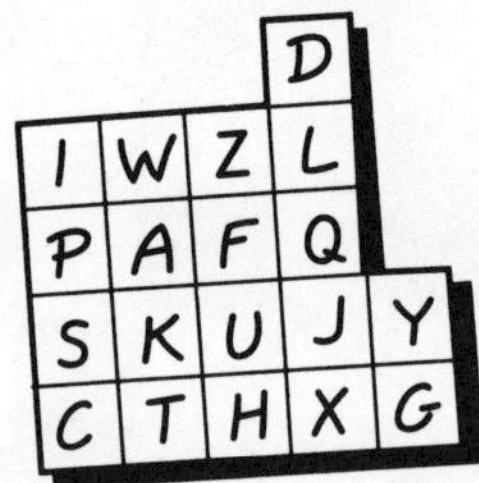
D
I W Z L
P A F Q
S K U J Y
C T H X G

D O
R A I
F P H Q N
S K B V E Z
C X W M T G

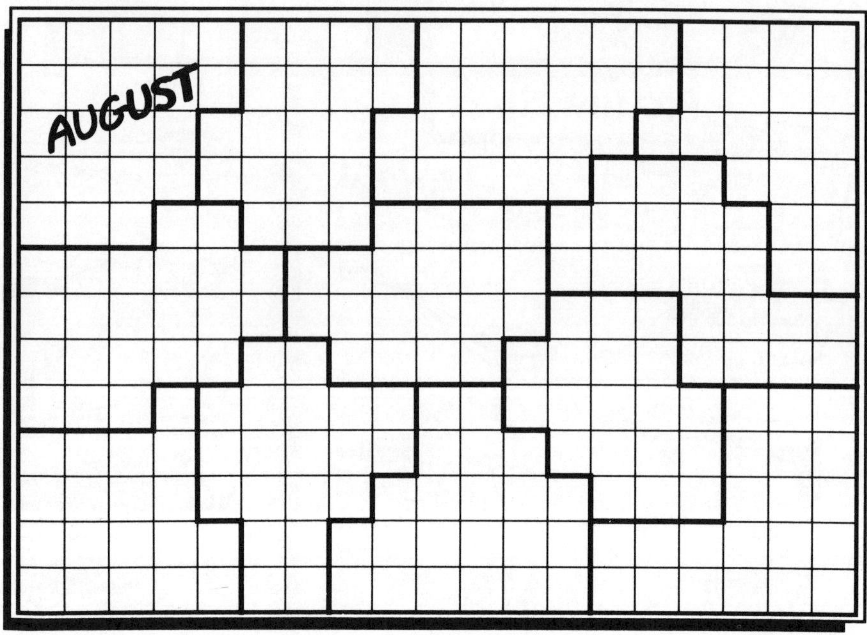
AUGUST

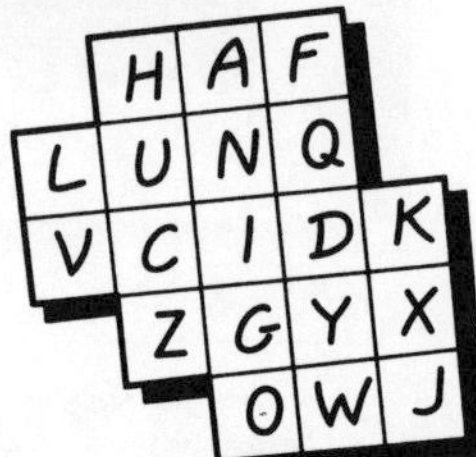
H A F
L U N Q
V C I D K
Z G Y X
O W J

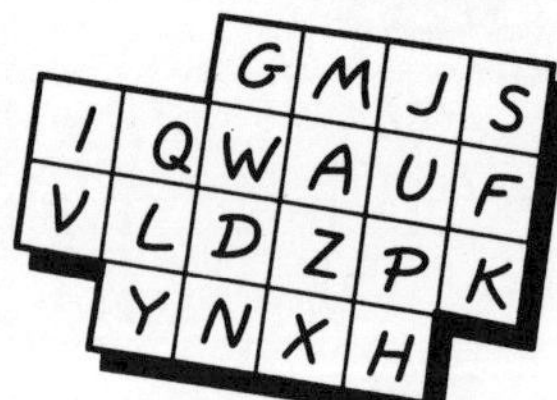
G M J S
I Q W A U F
V L D Z P K
Y N X H

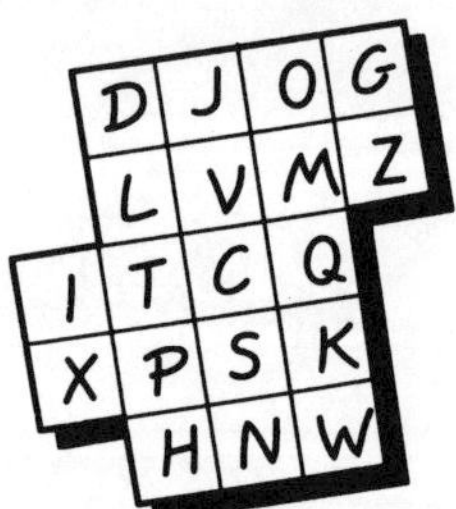
D J O G
L V M Z
I T C Q
X P S K
H N W

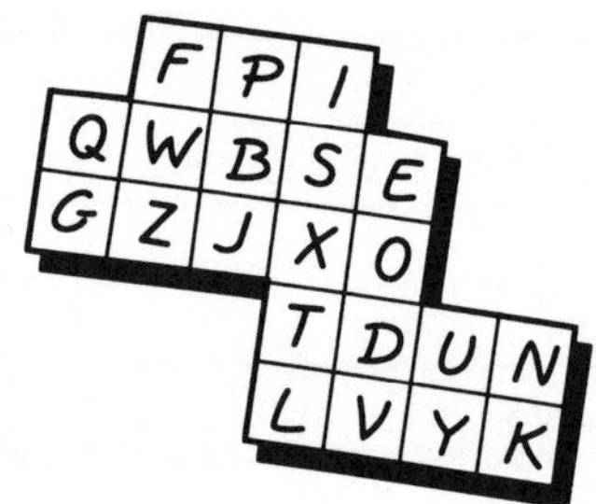
F P I
Q W B S E
G Z J X O
T D U N
L V Y K

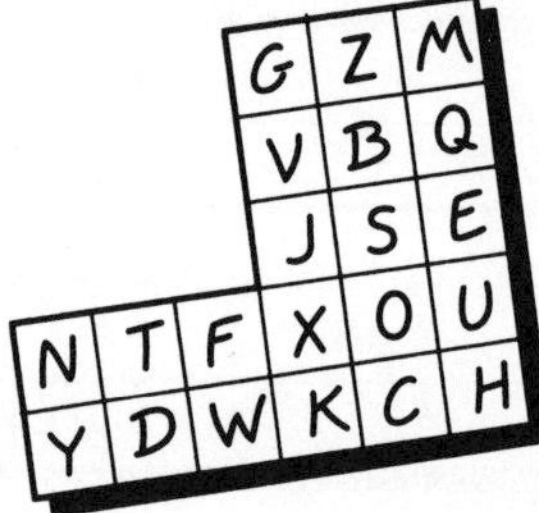
G Z M
V B Q
J S E
N T F X O U
Y D W K C H

I O L G
X U A S
T K N Y J
F P W
Z H
Q V

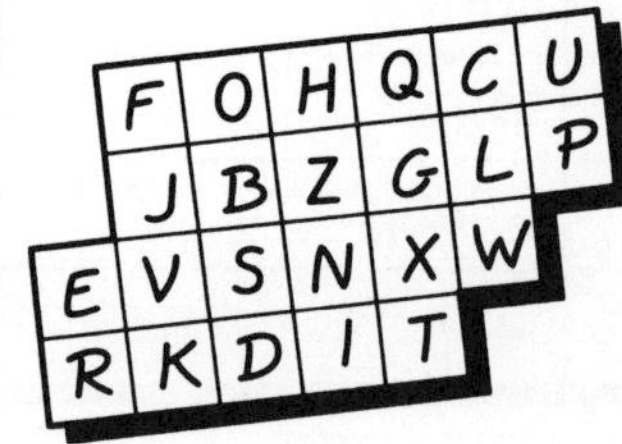
F O H Q C U
J B Z G L P
E V S N X W
R K D I T

Verb mini-crossword

For this crossword, the clues are groups of verbs. In each group of three verbs, find the one which does not rhyme with the other two. Put that verb into the grid.

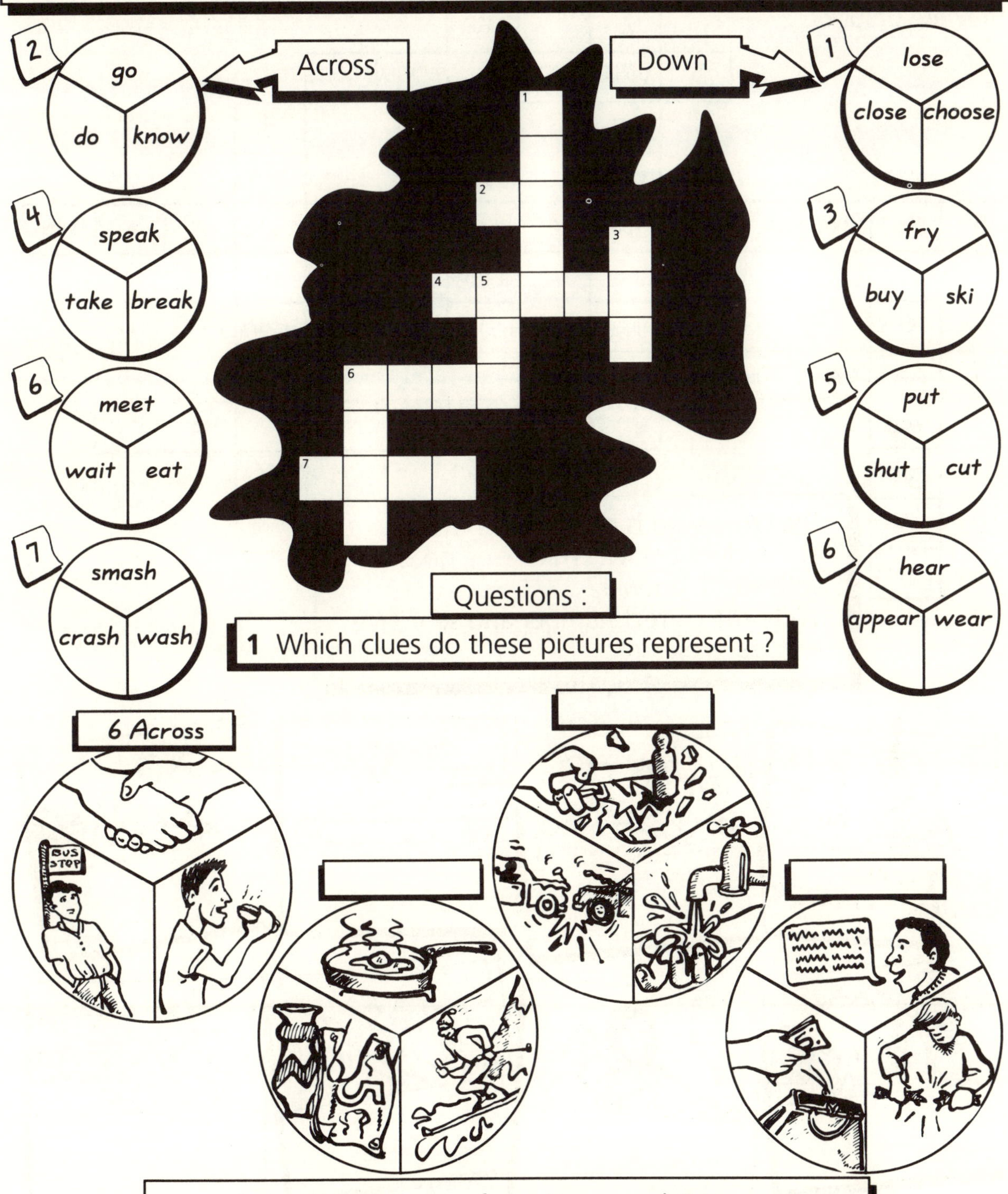

Across
2 go do know
4 speak take break
6 meet wait eat
7 smash crash wash
Down
1 lose close choose
3 fry buy ski
5 put shut cut
6 hear appear wear
1
2
3
4
5
6
7
Questions :
1 Which clues do these pictures represent ?
6 Across
BUS STOP

2 Look at the clues for *1 Down* and *5 Down*.
Of those six verbs, which two have the same meaning?

Don't do it - it's unlucky!

In the crossword there are eight superstitions. They are all things *not to do*, because they are unlucky.

1 DON'T CARRY AN AXE ON YOUR SHOULDER INDOORS

2 DON'T TALK WHEN YOU ARE UNDER A BRIDGE

3 DON'T OPEN AN UMBRELLA INDOORS

4 DON'T GO PAST ANOTHER PERSON ON THE STAIRS

5 DON'T LOOK BACK WHEN YOU LEAVE YOUR HOME TO GO ON A JOURNEY

6 DON'T WALK UNDER A LADDER

7 DON'T PUT SHOES ON A TABLE

8 DON'T WHISTLE ON A BOAT

The crossword is complete - but look at the clues below: which clue goes with which answer?
Write the correct number and sentence with each picture.

6
DON'T WALK
UNDER A LADDER

Question:

Do you have any of these superstitions in your country?

PHOTOCOPIABLE

CALCULATOR

Look at this number: three hundred and thirty-five

If you put it on a calculator:

335
7 8 9 0 ÷

and turn the calculator upside down,
you find an English verb:

SEE

Do the same with the other numbers on this page. They make some names, an adjective and some verbs. Use a calculator if you have one. If you don't have a calculator, you can still do the puzzle; fill in the parts of the numbers, like this:

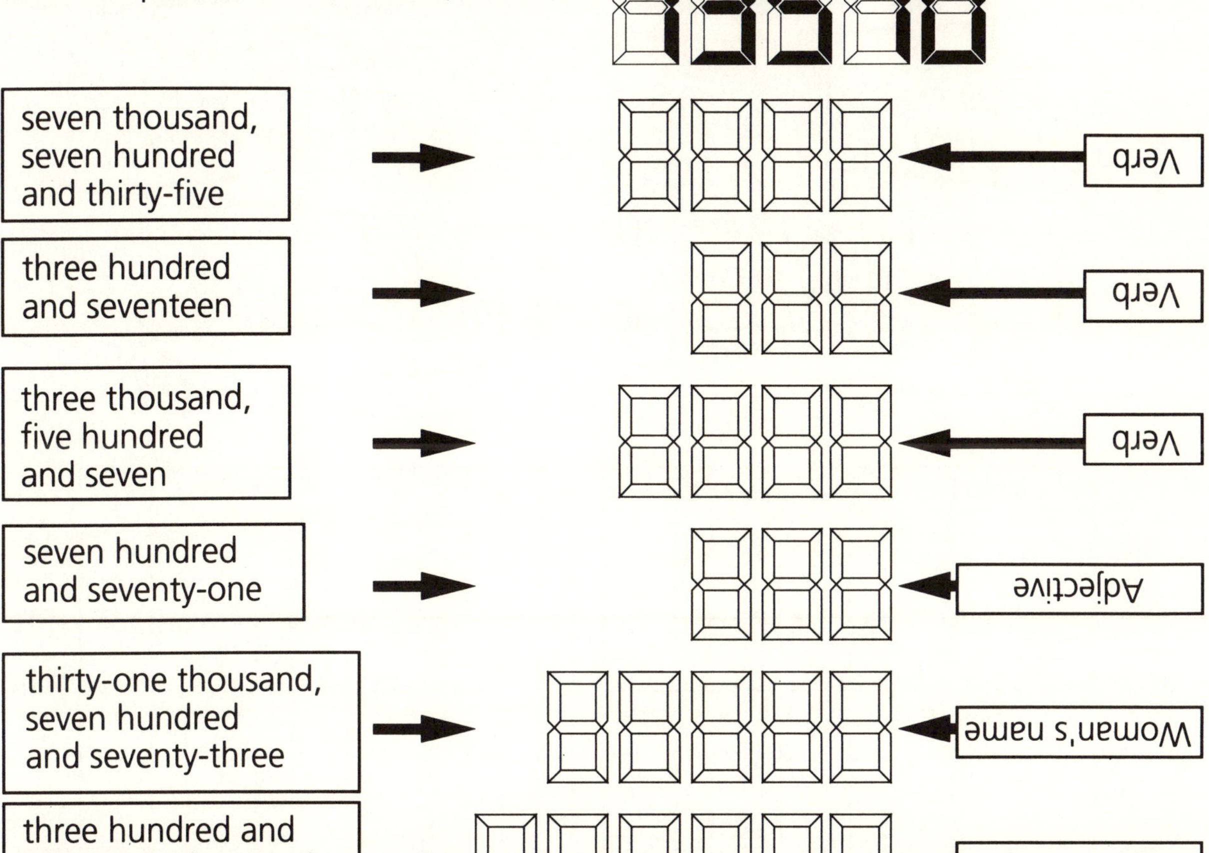

seven thousand, seven hundred and thirty-five
Verb
three hundred and seventeen
Verb
three thousand, five hundred and seven
Verb
seven hundred and seventy-one
Adjective
thirty-one thousand, seven hundred and seventy-three
Woman's name
three hundred and seventeen thousand, five hundred and thirty-seven
Man's name

PHOTOCOPIABLE

FOLDING DOORS

Look at this folding door.

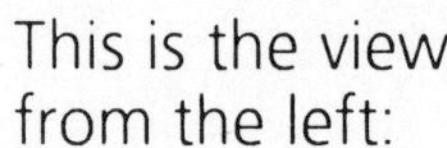
This is the view
from the left:

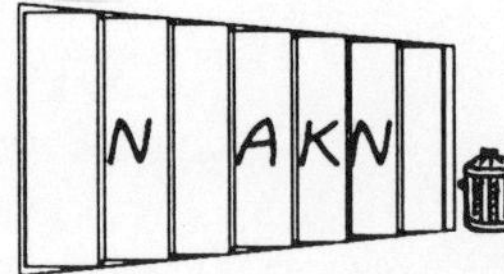
N AKN

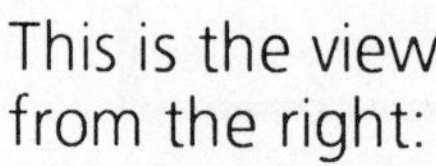
This is the view
from the right:

OPRIG

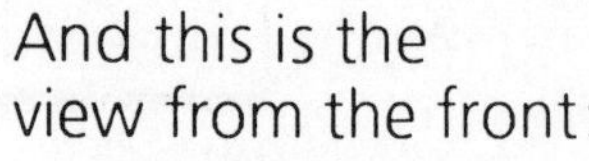
And this is the
view from the front:

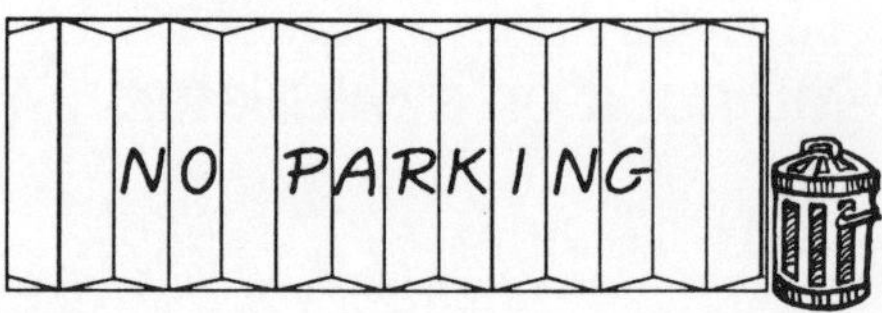
NO PARKING

Here are views of four more doors, from the left and from the right. Discover what is written on them:

Write the words on these front views:

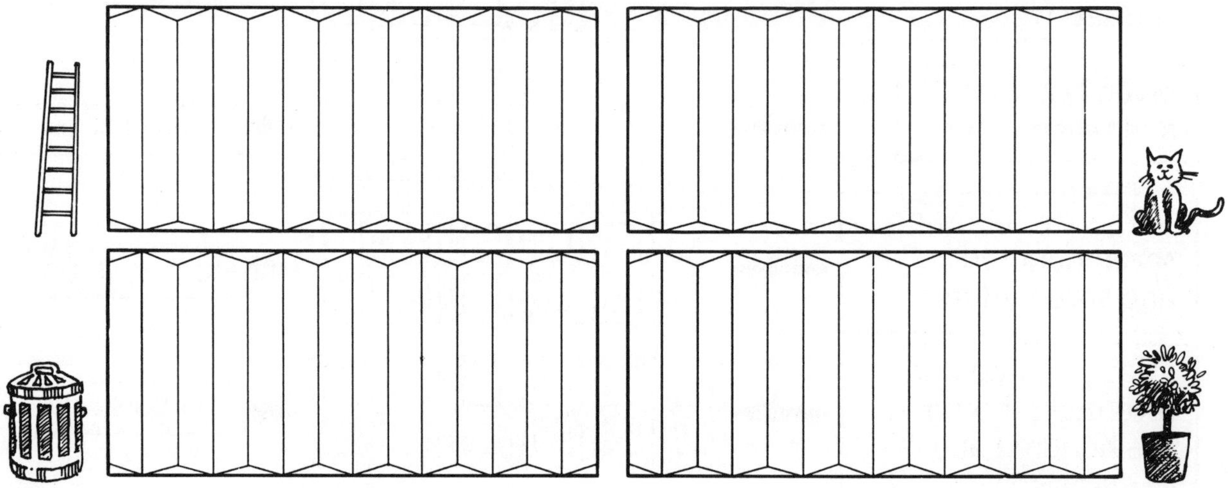

PHOTOCOPIABLE

LONGER, SHORTER

In this puzzle, from the first answer to the third answer, the words get longer.
Number 1 has two letters; Number 2 has those two letters - and one more;
Number 3 has those three letters - and one more.
Then, from the third answer to the fifth answer, the words get shorter.

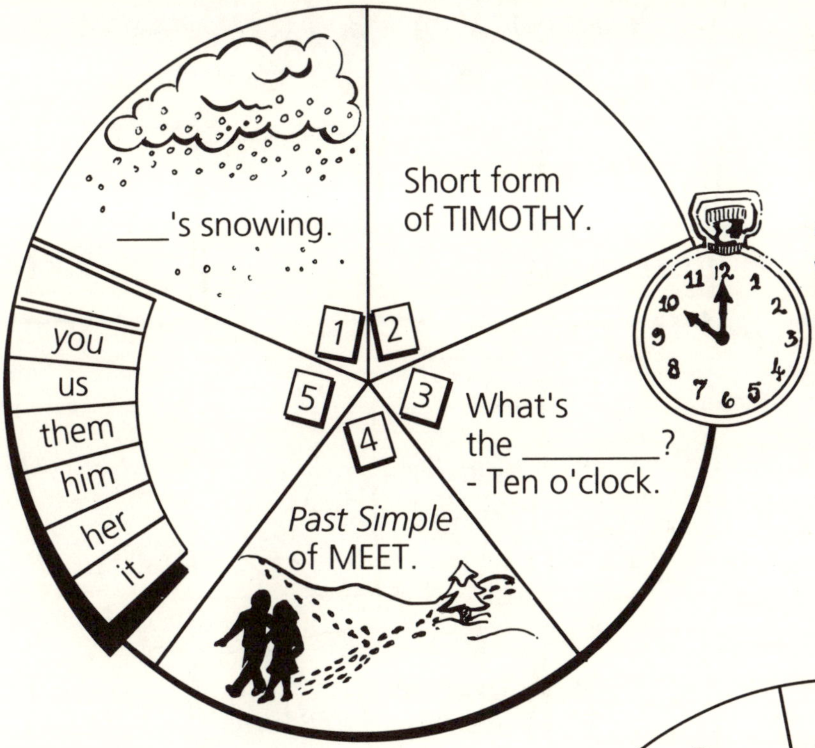

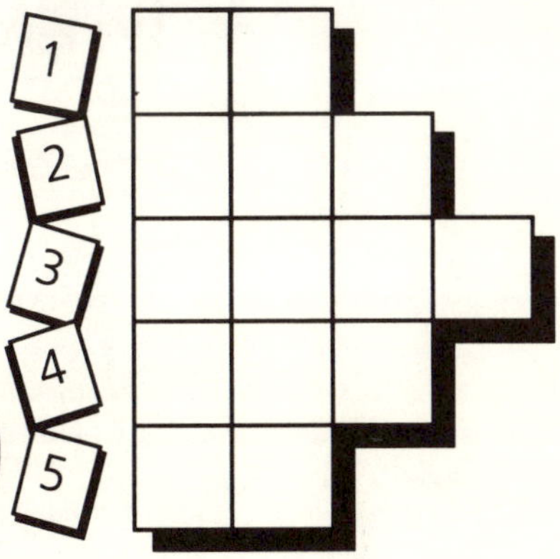

1. ___'s snowing.
2. Short form of TIMOTHY.
3. What's the ________? - Ten o'clock.
4. *Past Simple* of MEET.
5. you / us / them / him / her / it

Do this puzzle in the same way:

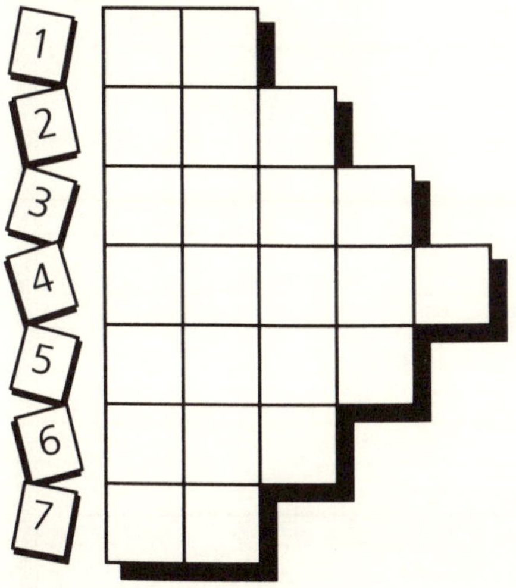

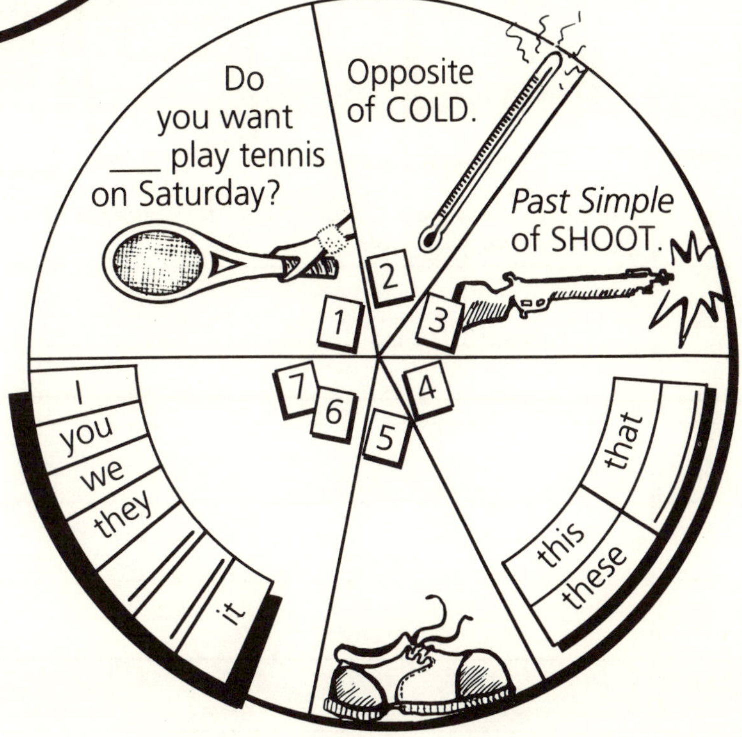

1. Do you want ___ play tennis on Saturday?
2. Opposite of COLD.
3. *Past Simple* of SHOOT.
4. this / that / these
5.
6.
7. I / you / we / they / it

PHOTOCOPIABLE

IDENTITY PARADE

Assemble a sentence about each person by taking a piece from each of the three groups.

1
2
3
4
5
6
7

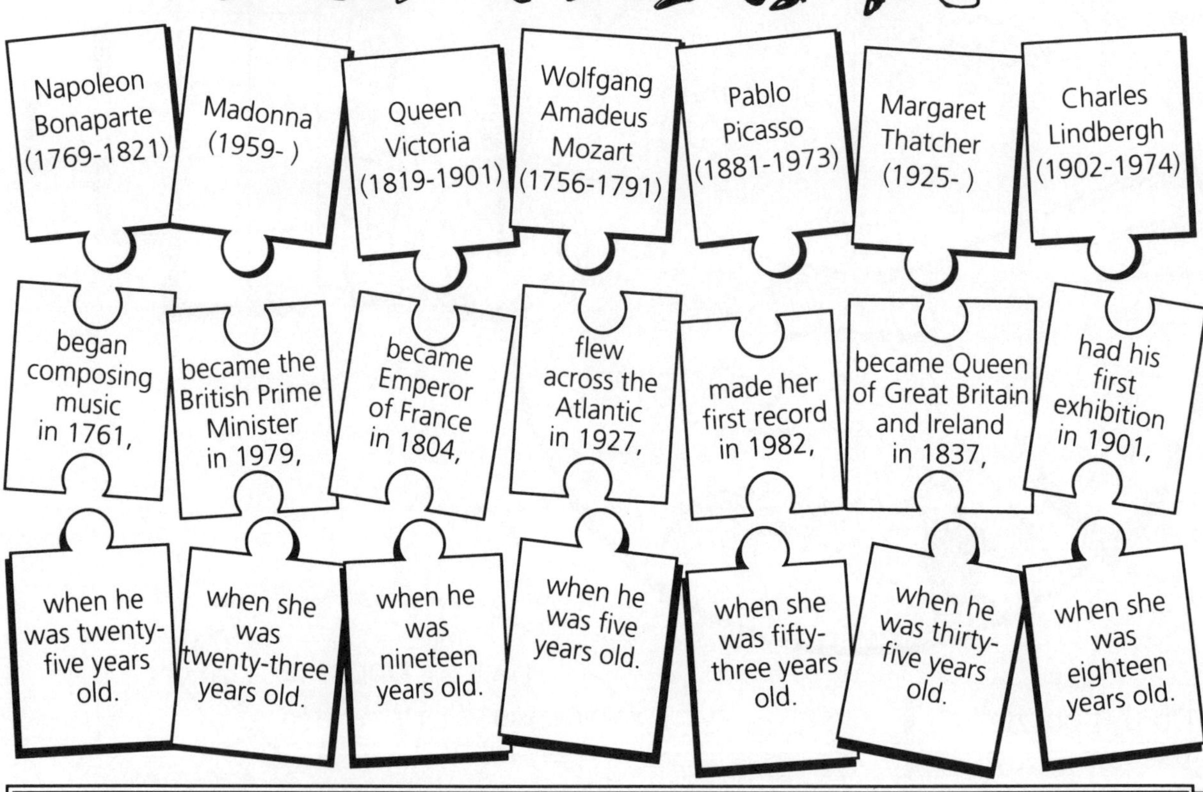
Napoleon Bonaparte (1769-1821)
Madonna (1959-)
Queen Victoria (1819-1901)
Wolfgang Amadeus Mozart (1756-1791)
Pablo Picasso (1881-1973)
Margaret Thatcher (1925-)
Charles Lindbergh (1902-1974)
began composing music in 1761,
became the British Prime Minister in 1979,
became Emperor of France in 1804,
flew across the Atlantic in 1927,
made her first record in 1982,
became Queen of Great Britain and Ireland in 1837,
had his first exhibition in 1901,
when he was twenty-five years old.
when she was twenty-three years old.
when he was nineteen years old.
when he was five years old.
when she was fifty-three years old.
when he was thirty-five years old.
when she was eighteen years old.

1	*Charles Lindbergh (1902-1974) flew across the Atlantic in 1927, when he was twenty-five years old.*
2	
3	
4	
5	
6	
7	

PHOTOCOPIABLE

Find the Family

This family of words has seven members: 'MY' is the first.
What are the six others? Like 'MY', each is hidden in a place name.
Can you find them?

1
WEMBLEY STADIUM
2
SYDNEY HARBOUR BRIDGE
3
HADRIAN'S WALL
4
THE TOWER OF LONDON
5
VICTORIA FALLS
6
MOUNT EVEREST
7
THE EIFFEL TOWER

1 MY

2

3

4

5

6

7

CLOTHES

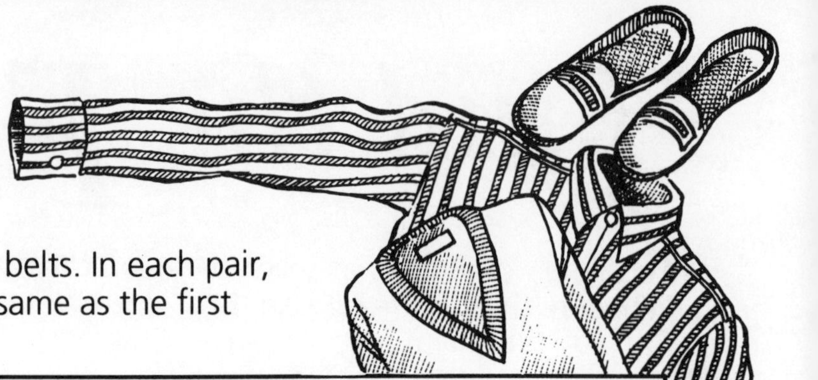

Put the pairs of words on the correct belts. In each pair, the last letter of the first word is the same as the first letter of the second word.

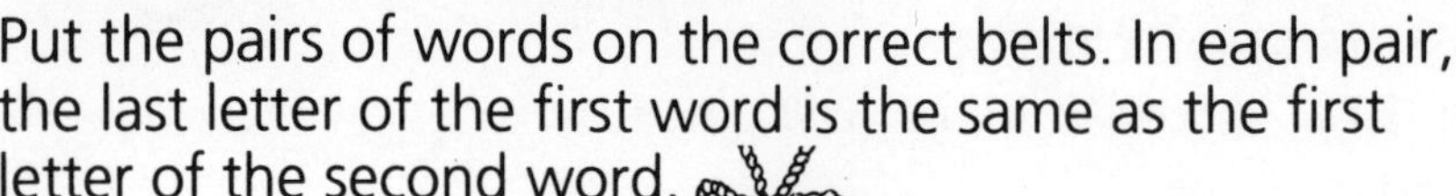

For example:

HAT
TIE

H A T I E

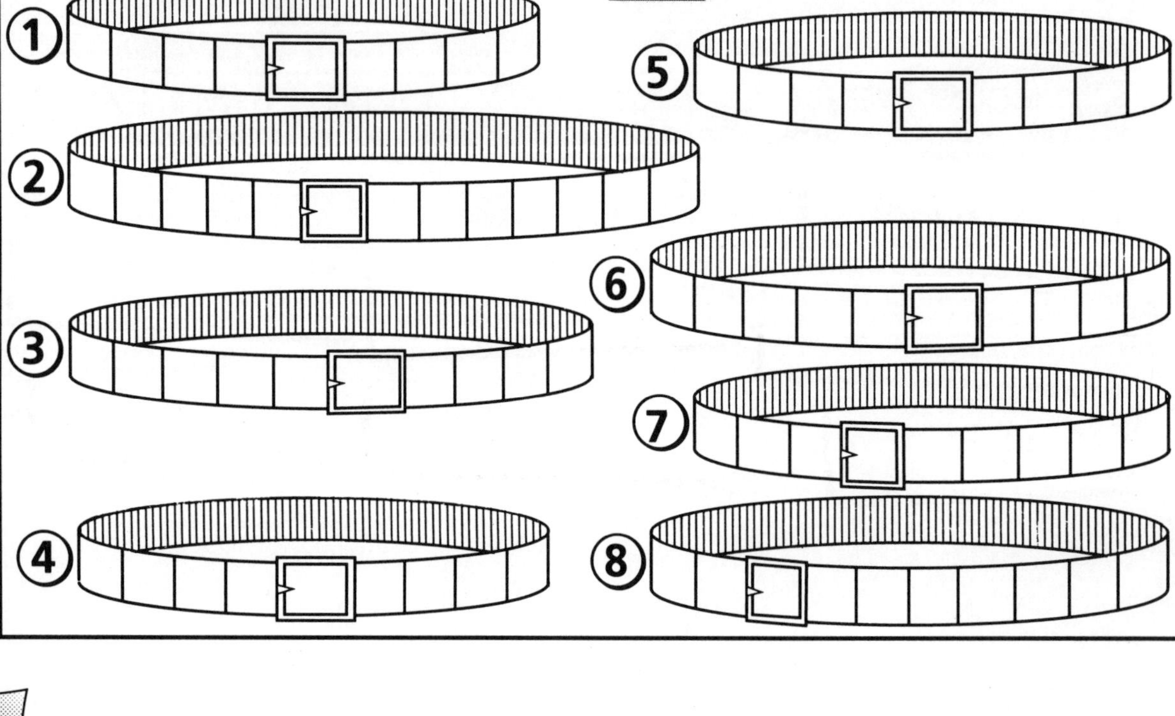

PHOTOCOPIABLE

ELVIS'S GREATEST HITS

In this puzzle, there are ten Elvis Presley songs. The title of each song is two words.

1 Assemble these seven titles and write them with the correct pictures.

GUITAR
KENTUCKY
LITTLE
LOVE
ONE
TEDDY
WOODEN
BEAR
HEART
LETTERS
MAN
RAIN
NIGHT
SISTER
KE KY
GUITAR MAN

2 Put those seven titles into this grid, horizontally.

	a	b	c	d	e	f	g	h	i	j	k	l	m
1													
2													
3													
4													
5	G	U	I	T	A	R		M	A	N			
6													
7													

3 Find three more titles by taking the correct letters from the grid.

6g	3a	5b	2c		5h	3b	1c	4m

6g	7e	4e	6b		6j	2f	3c	7f	3k

6g	3f	5b	3j		4f	2h	1k	5c	7j	3i	5h	1j	3l

A + B = C

Write the words under the pictures in Groups A and B. (The words are in the boxes, but the letters are in the wrong order.) Then put together a word from Group A and a word from Group B to make each word in Group C.

Group A

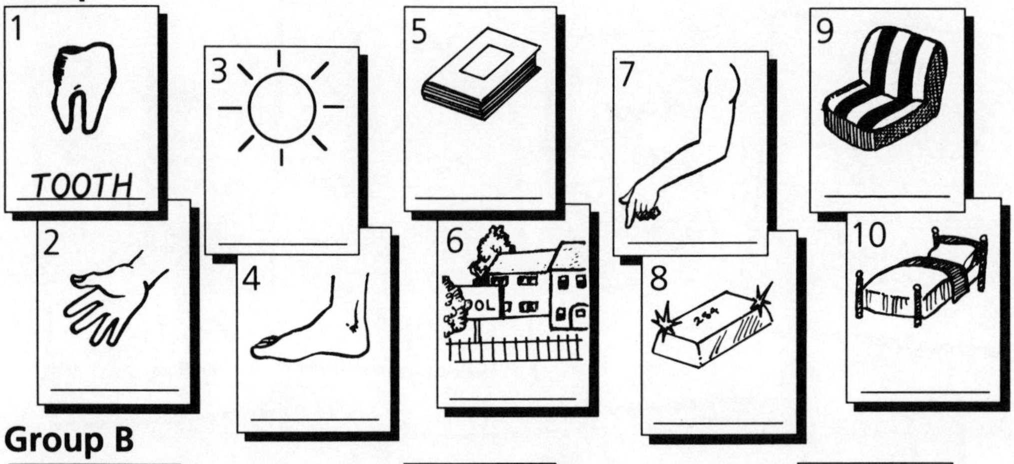

1 TOOTH

2

3

4

5

6

7

8

9

10

DBE
UNS
RMA
KOBO
HTOTO
OGDL
LSHOCO
TOOF
NADH
STAE

Group B

HCIRA
UHBRS
SIHF
LLBA
MORO
LTEB
PHSO
OYB
ELFWOR
GBA

11

12

13 BRUSH

14

15

16

17

18

19

20

Group C

21 TOOTHBRUSH

22

23

24

25

26

27

28

29

30

PHOTOCOPIABLE

MISTAKES AT THE AIRPORT

In each of the signs, there is a spelling mistake (an extra letter). For each one, correct the mistake and put the extra letter in the small square.

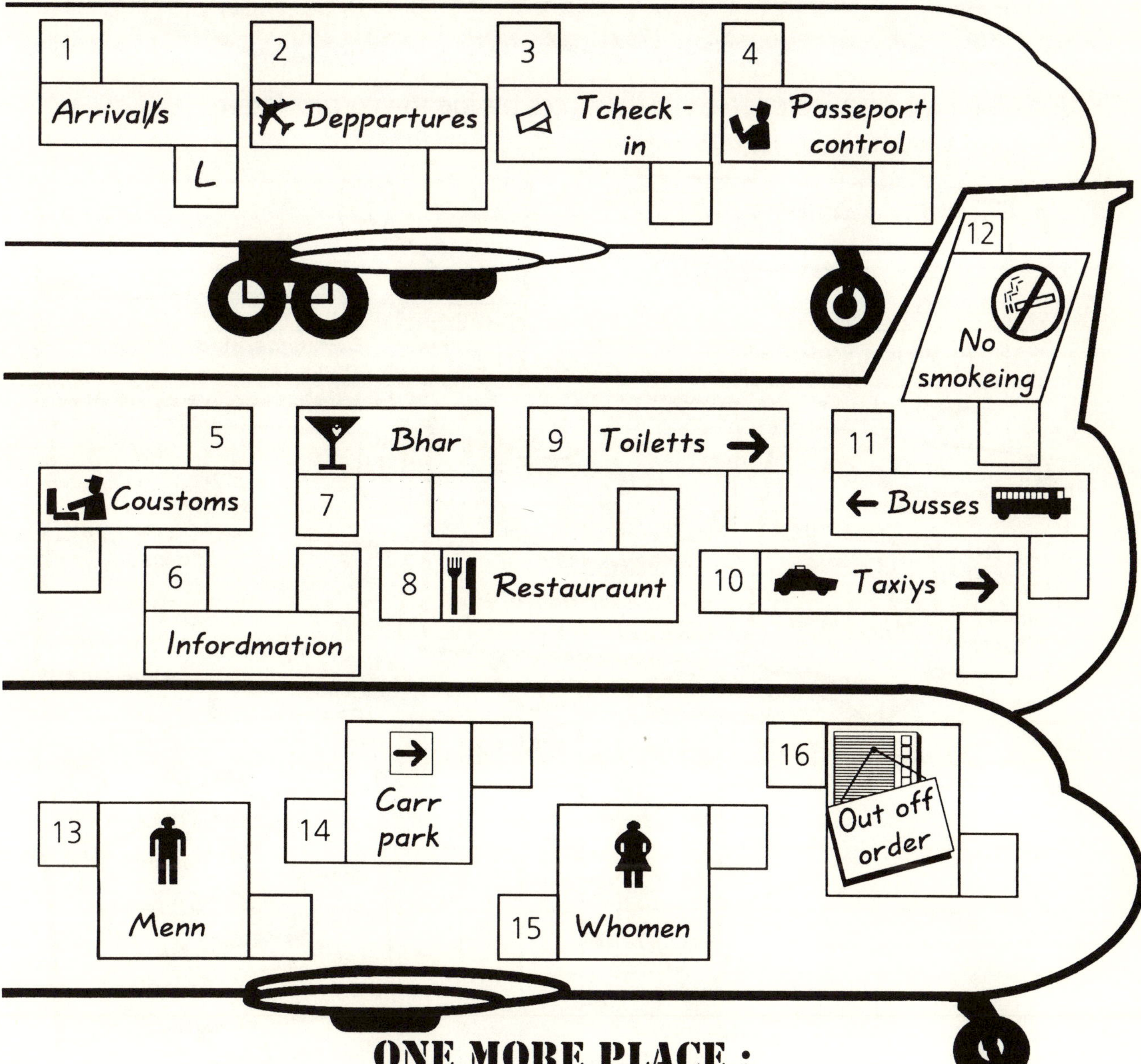

1
Arrivalls
L
2
Deppartures
3
Tcheck - in
4
Passeport control
12
No smokeing
5
Coustoms
Bhar
7
9
Toiletts
11
Busses
6
Infordmation
8
Restauraunt
10
Taxiys
16
Out off order
13
Menn
14
Carr park
15
Whomen

ONE MORE PLACE :

Put the correct letters in these squares, to spell another place you could find at an airport.

6	8	9	10		16	14	4	12		11	7	5	2
				-					■				

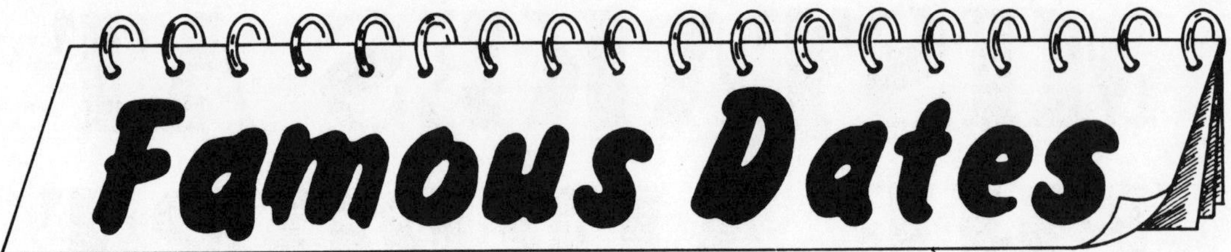
Famous Dates

Here are six famous dates:

21st July 1969 | 2nd March 1969 | 20th July 1969 | 12th April 1961 | 24th August 1939 | 17th December 1903

With the help of the pictures, put the dates beside the correct letters.

1900 Write each date in two ways.

A: The Wright brothers made the first plane flight (Kittyhawk, N.Carolina, USA).

D: Concorde made its first flight (Toulouse, France).

1965

B: The first jet plane, the Heinkel He 178, made its first flight (Rostock - Marienehe, Germany).

C: Yuri Gagarin orbited the Earth in **Vostok 1**.

E: **Apollo 11** landed on the moon.

1950

F: Neil Armstrong walked on the moon.

2000

Date		Letter		Day	Month	Year
17th December 1903	←	A	→	17	12	03
	←	B	→			
	←	C	→			
	←	D	→			
	←	E	→			
	←	F	→			

If your numbers are correct, these calculations are correct:

□ + □ = □ + □

□ + □ = □ + □

PHOTOCOPIABLE

LONGER, SHORTER, LONGER...

In this puzzle, from the first answer to the fourth answer, the words get longer. Number 1 has two letters; Number 2 has those two letters – and one more; Number 3 has those three letters – and one more. After Number 4 the words get shorter; after Number 7 they get longer, etc.

1 Where's Glasgow? - It's __ Scotland.
2
3 Short form of CHRISTINA.
4
5
6 Past Simple of RUN.
7 I'm ___ air hostess.
8
9 I don't understand this word. What does it _____?
10 JOHN SUSAN ANGELA JACK
11 Opposite of DIFFERENT.
12 Short form of SAMUEL.
13 _____ is are
14
15 I'm a vegetarian. I don't eat _______.
16 This bridge is made of _______.
17 Opposite of EARLY.
18
19 I got up ___ seven o'clock this morning.
20 Past Simple of 24.
21 _____ and pepper.
22
23 1. 2. 3. 4. 5. 6. 7.
24 Can I _____ here?
25 am _______ are
26 my your our ____ their her its
27 ____ that these those
28
1 I N
2
3
4
5
6
7
8
9
10
11
12
13
14
15
16
17
18
19
20
21
22
23
24
25
26
27
28

Solutions

Coloured Pens

Page 7

1. BLACK
2. YELLOW
3. ORANGE
4. RED
5. GREY
6. BLUE
7. WHITE
8. GREEN
9. BROWN

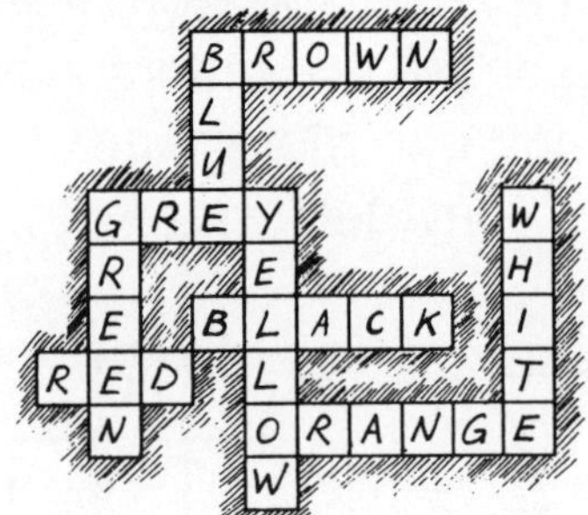
BROWN
BLUE
GREY
WHITE
YELLOW
BLACK
RED
GREEN
ORANGE

Film Titles

Page 8

1. Seven Angry Men
2. Three Men on a Horse
3. Two Women
4. Seven Women
5. Three Men in a Boat
6. Two People
7. Ten Tall Men
8. Twelve Angry Men

Shopping Accident

Page 9

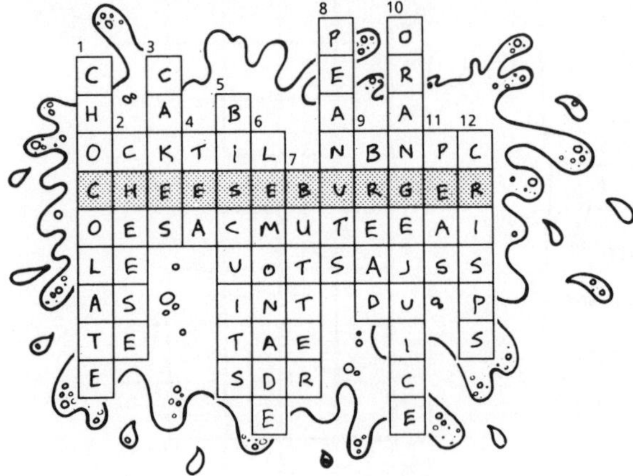
CHEESEBURGER

American Football

Page 10

Number One's name is WASHINGTON.
Number Three's name is JEFFERSON.
Number Seven's name is JACKSON.
Number Twelve's name is TAYLOR.
Number Twenty-eight's name is WILSON.
Number Thirty-seven's name is NIXON.
Number Forty's name is REAGAN.
Number Forty-one's name is BUSH.

Those names are names of American presidents: George *Washington*, Thomas *Jefferson*, Andrew *Jackson*, Zachary *Taylor*, Woodrow *Wilson*, Richard *Nixon*, Ronald *Reagan*, George *Bush*. Washington was the 1st president, Jefferson was the 3rd, Jackson was the 7th, etc.

Find the Words

Page 11

Only the words in the grey squares have *an* – these are words beginning with A, E, I, O, U (when it is not pronounced /ju:/), and silent H.

B a bottle
C a cassette
G a glove
A an apple
D a door
F a fish

J a jacket
E an eye
M a motorbike
N a nest
K a key
L a lamp
H an hour
H a hand
I an insect
P a plane
Q a queue
R a ruler
S a sandwich
O an orange
X a xylophone
Z a zebra
U a uniform
U an umbrella
W a watch
V a violin
Y a yacht
T a table

Wind Damage

Page 12

1. CINEMA
2. RESTAURANT
3. BANK
4. HOTEL
5. SWIMMING POOL
6. BOOKSHOP
7. SCHOOL
8. POST OFFICE
9. SUPERMARKET
10. NEWSAGENT

Crossword Pieces

Page 13

							F			
			S	A	T	U	R	D	A	Y
					U		I			
	W	E	D	N	E	S	D	A	Y	
					S		A			
T	H	U	R	S	D	A	Y			
					A					
M	O	N	D	A	Y					

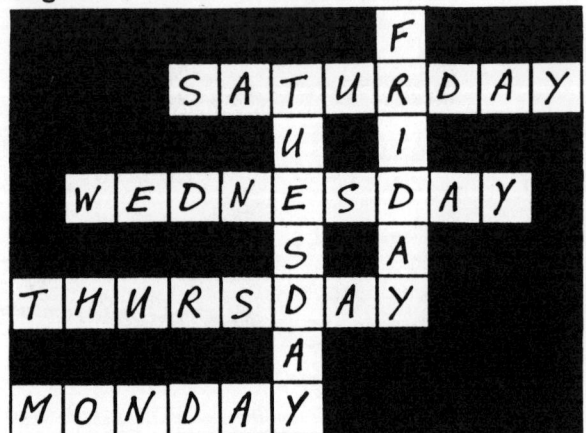

The missing day is SUNDAY.

Male and Female

Page 14

Crossword B

AUNT
PRINCESS
WIFE
DAUGHTER
QUEEN MOTHER
SISTER
WOMAN
GIRL

Add a Letter

Page 15

BUS → BUSH
EAT → EAST
CAR → CARD
TIN → THIN
RAIN → TRAIN
HAIR → CHAIR
TREE → THREE
LOVE → GLOVE
READ → BREAD

AT → HAT
ON → ONE
TO → TWO
DO → DOG
NOW → SNOW
OUR → HOUR
ALL → TALL
OTHER → MOTHER

Names

Page 16

1. LIZ
2. BILL
3. TOM
4. MIKE
5. PETE
6. SUE
7. BOB
8. DAN
9. DAVE

1 ELIZABETH, 2 WILLIAM, 3 THOMAS, 4 MICHAEL, 5 PETER, 6 SUSAN, 7 ROBERT, 8 DANIEL, 9 DAVID

Theatre Posters

Page 17

1. MEN WITHOUT SHADOWS
2. HAPPY DAYS
3. THE BIRDS
4. THE FROGS
5. ALL MY SONS
6. THREE SISTERS
7. THE FLIES
8. THE LITTLE FOXES

Remember:
Most nouns make their plural by adding s to the singular (birds, sisters, sons, frogs, shadows). This includes nouns ending with a vowel + *y* (days).
Nouns ending with a consonant +*y* make their plural with *ies* (fly – flies).
Nouns ending with *x*, *s*, *ch* or *sh* make their plural with *es* (foxes).
Some nouns have irregular plurals (man – men).

Do-It-Yourself

Page 18

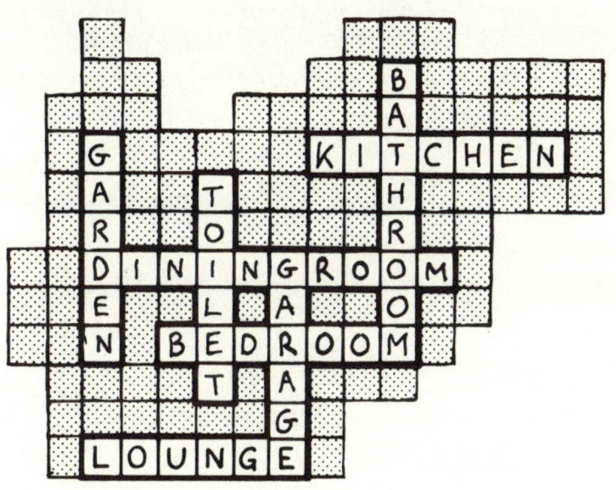

BATHROOM
KITCHEN
GARDEN
TOILET
DINING ROOM
BEDROOM
GARAGE
LOUNGE

At the Cinema

Page 19

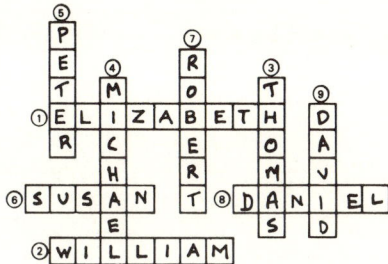

Mr Smith Goes To Washington	Queen Christina
The Man From Morocco	The Little Princess
Uncle Silas	Mrs Miniver
The Boy With Green Hair	My Daughter Joy
My Son John	Aunt Clara
A King In New York	Good Morning, Miss Dove
Goodbye, Mr Chips	My Sister Eileen
Brother John	A Girl Named Tamiko
The Boyfriend	An Unmarried Woman
The Little Prince	The Good Mother

A Different Alphabet

Page 20

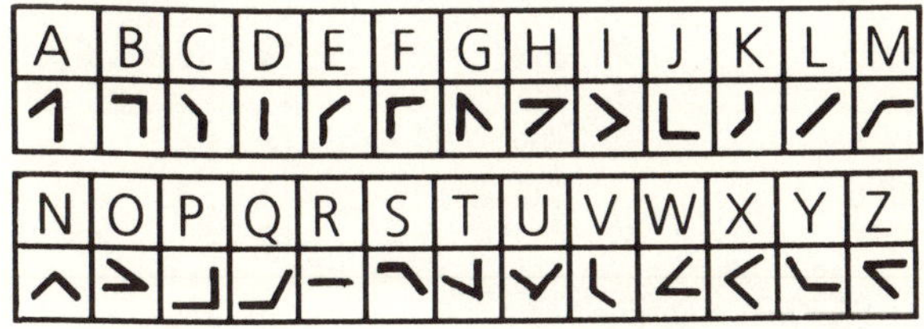

A B C D E F G H I J K L M
N O P Q R S T U V W X Y Z

1. LIBRARY
2. TAXIS
3. JAZZ CLUB
4. SWEETSHOP
5. MARKET SQUARE
6. HEALTH CENTRE
7. SHAKESPEARE AVENUE

In fact, those symbols show the positions of the flags in the semaphore alphabet:

A B etc.

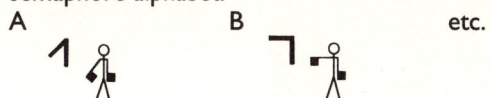

Countries in Code

Page 21

AYILT → ITALY
NSIAP → SPAIN
ANAPJ → JAPAN
ZRLBAI → BRAZIL
CFNEAR → FRANCE
ADACNA → CANADA
NAGMEYR → GERMANY
PATUOGRL → PORTUGAL

At Home

Page 22

1. COOKER
2. BED
3. SOFA
4. TELEVISION
5. FRIDGE
6. BATH
7. ARMCHAIR
8. BOOKCASE
9. TABLE
10. CHAIR
11. RECORD-PLAYER
12. WINDOW

Proverbs:
Home is where the heart is.
There's no place like home.
East, west, home is best.

Book Titles

Page 23

The House in Paris Elizabeth Bowen
A Fire On The Moon Norman Mailer
Our Man In Havana Graham Greene
To The Lighthouse Virginia Woolf
Just Above My Head James Baldwin
A Small Town in Germany John le Carré
Under The Volcano Malcolm Lowry
Across The River And Into The Trees Ernest Hemingway
A Flag On The Island V. S. Naipaul
The Waves Behind The Boat Francis King

Verb Crossword

Page 24

1. BEGIN
2. PLAY
3. WASH
4. RELAX
5. PULL
6. BORROW
7. ASK
8. PAY
9. FINISH
10. STOP
11. LISTEN
12. PUSH
13. CARRY
14. WATCH
15. WALK
16. SAY
17. EAT
18. GO

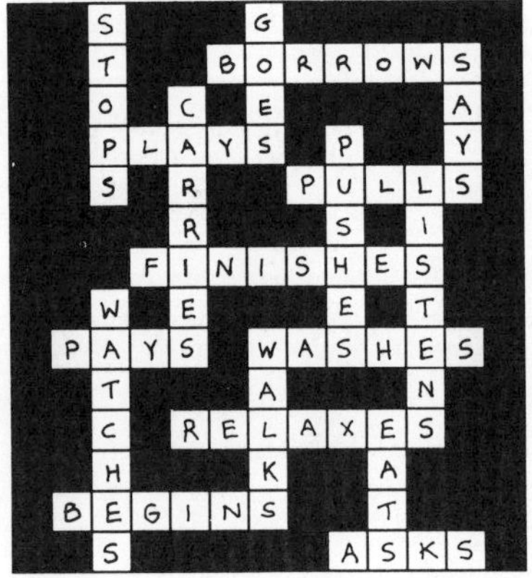

Remember:
Most verbs add s (begins, pulls, borrows, asks, stops, listens, walks, eats). This includes verbs ending with a vowel +y (plays, pays, says).
Verbs ending with a consonant +y use *ies* (carry – carries).
Verbs ending with *x, s, ch, sh* or *o* add es (washes, relaxes, finishes, pushes, watches, goes).

Add Two Letters

Page 25

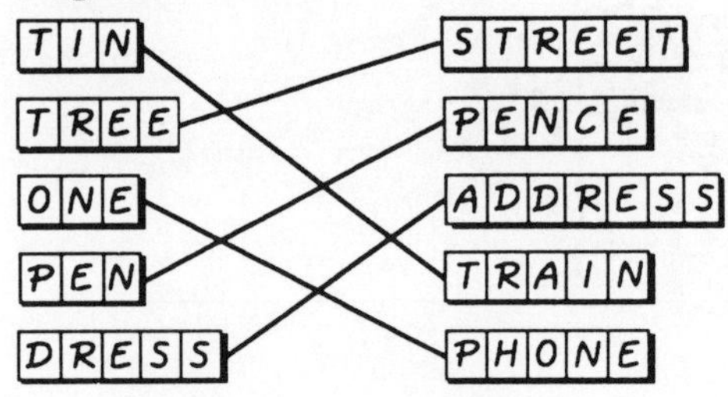
TIN
TREE
ONE
PEN
DRESS
STREET
PENCE
ADDRESS
TRAIN
PHONE

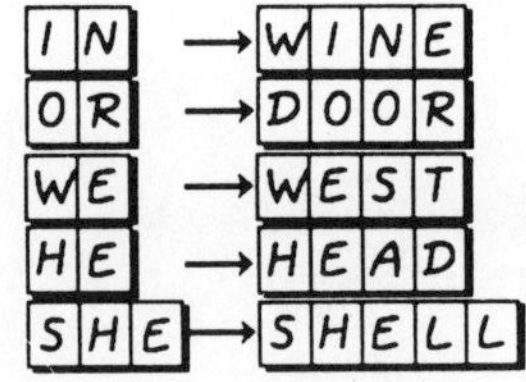
IN → WINE
OR → DOOR
WE → WEST
HE → HEAD
SHE → SHELL

TV Programmes

Page 26

9 ACROSS
11 DOWN
4 DOWN
10 ACROSS
3 DOWN
1 DOWN
6 ACROSS
12 ACROSS
2 ACROSS
2 DOWN
8 DOWN
7 ACROSS
4 ACROSS
7 DOWN
5 DOWN

Jobs

Page 27

2
REPORTER
RFEPIORRETEMRAN
FIREMAN
3
AIR HOSTESS
APIORHLIOCSETESMASN
POLICEMAN
4
POLICEWOMAN
PBOALINKCEWCOLMAENRK
BANK CLERK
5
SHOP ASSISTANT
SSHOEPACSRSIESTTAANRTY
SECRETARY

Song Titles
Page 28

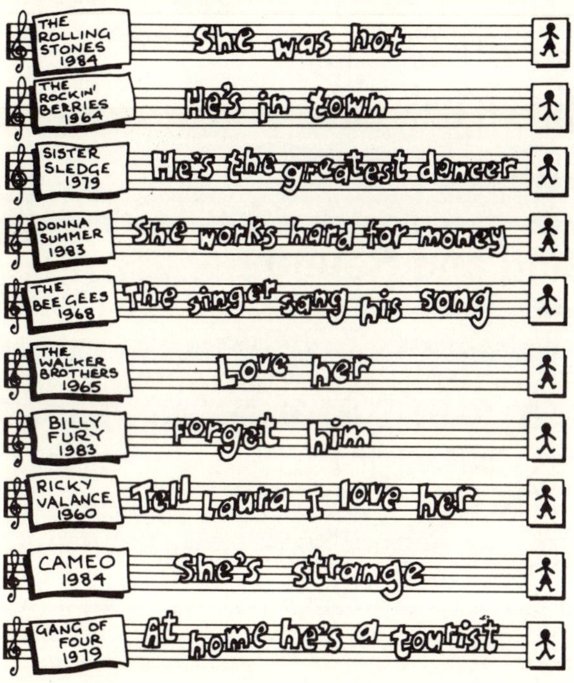

THE ROLLING STONES 1984
She was hot
THE ROCKIN' BERRIES 1964
He's in town
SISTER SLEDGE 1979
He's the greatest dancer
DONNA SUMMER 1983
She works hard for money
THE BEE GEES 1968
The singer sang his song
THE WALKER BROTHERS 1965
Love her
BILLY FURY 1983
Forget him
RICKY VALANCE 1960
Tell Laura I love her
CAMEO 1984
She's strange
GANG OF FOUR 1979
At home he's a tourist

Badges
Page 29

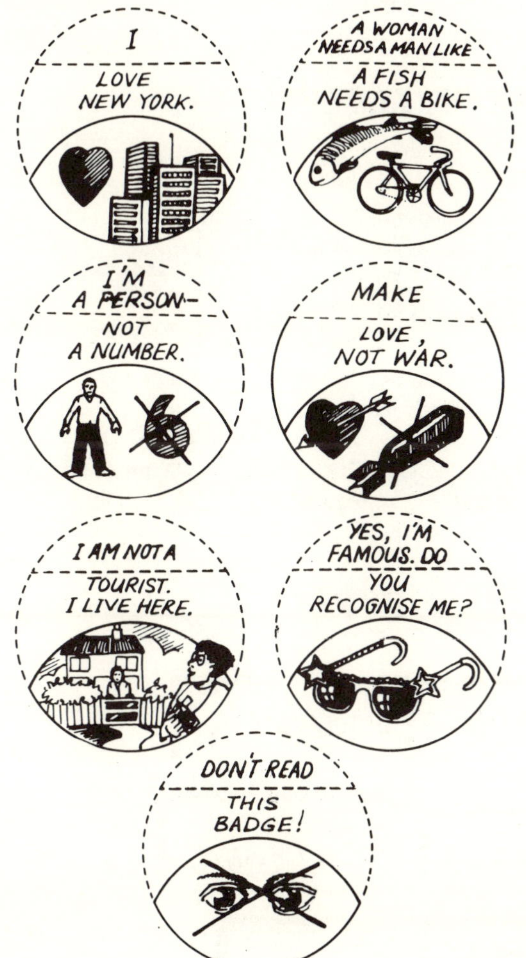

I LOVE NEW YORK.
A WOMAN NEEDS A MAN LIKE A FISH NEEDS A BIKE.
I'M A PERSON – NOT A NUMBER.
MAKE LOVE, NOT WAR.
I AM NOT A TOURIST. I LIVE HERE.
YES, I'M FAMOUS. DO YOU RECOGNISE ME?
DON'T READ THIS BADGE!

Verb backgammon
Page 30

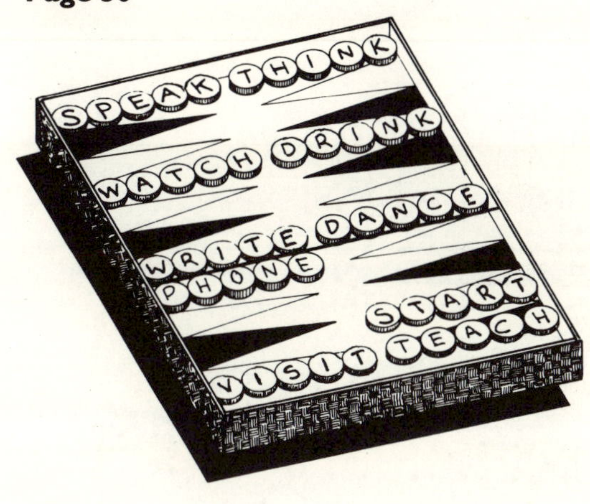

SPEAK THINK
WATCH DRINK
WRITE DANCE
PHONE
START
VISIT TEACH

Fruit
Page 31

1. KIWI FRUIT
2. BANANA
3. LEMON
4. PEAR
5. CHERRY
6. AVOCADO
7. STRAWBERRY
8. MELON
9. PINEAPPLE
10. COCONUT

Proverb: An apple a day keeps the doctor away.

Mistakes on the Signpost
Page 32

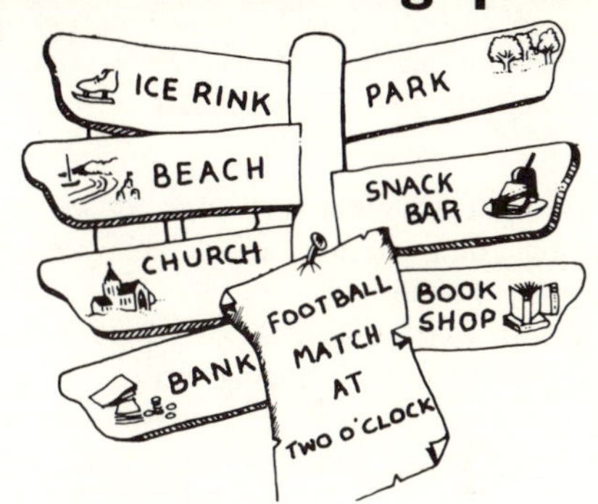

ICE RINK
PARK
BEACH
SNACK BAR
CHURCH
FOOTBALL MATCH AT TWO O'CLOCK
BOOK SHOP
BANK

Pounds and Pence
Page 33

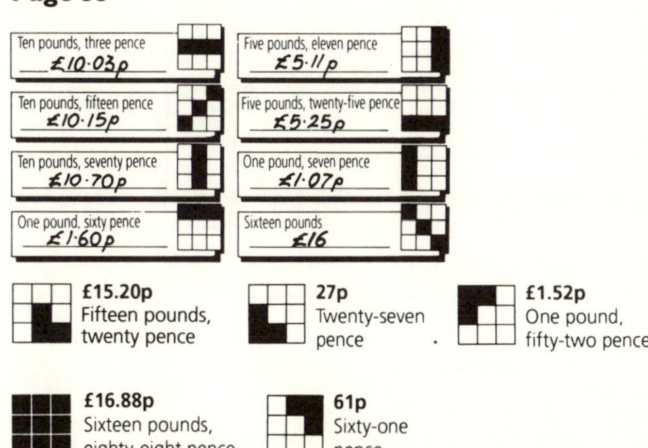

Ten pounds, three pence
£10·03p
Five pounds, eleven pence
£5·11p
Ten pounds, fifteen pence
£10·15p
Five pounds, twenty-five pence
£5·25p
Ten pounds, seventy pence
£10·70p
One pound, seven pence
£1·07p
One pound, sixty pence
£1·60p
Sixteen pounds
£16
£15.20p
Fifteen pounds, twenty pence
27p
Twenty-seven pence
£1.52p
One pound, fifty-two pence
£16.88p
Sixteen pounds, eighty-eight pence
61p
Sixty-one pence

Remember: In conversation, we often say, for example, 'Fifteen pounds, twenty' or 'Fifteen twenty' instead of 'Fifteen pounds, twenty pence'.

Musical Instruments

Page 34

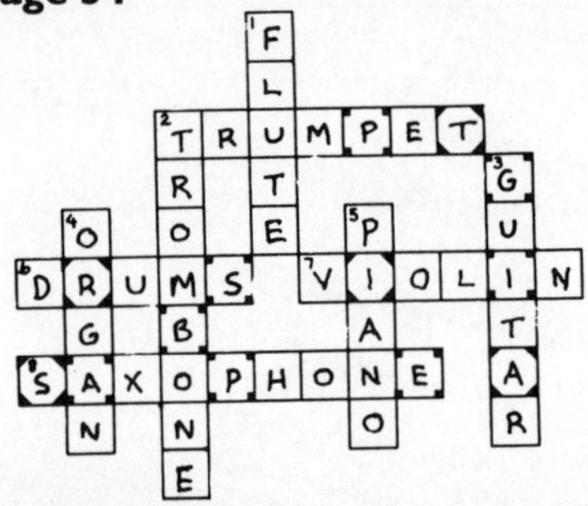

TRUMPET
DRUMS
VIOLIN
SAXOPHONE
FLUTE
TROMBONE
GUITAR
ORGAN
PIANO

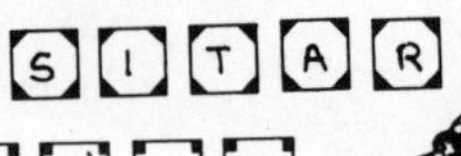

SITAR

BAGPIPES

Write the Clues

Page 35

Across
1. STUDY
4. SPELL
6. GET
7. START
9. LEAVE
10. SWIM
12. GO
14. TAKE
15. HOPE
16. OPEN

Down
2. TELL
3. DO
5. EAT
7. SKATE
8. RUN
9. LISTEN
11. WORK
13. STOP
15. HELP

To make their *ing*-form, most verbs just add *ing* (studying, spelling, starting, going, opening, telling, doing, eating, listening, working, helping).
Verbs ending with a consonant +e lose the e (leave – leaving, take – taking, hope – hoping, skate – skating).
Some verbs double the final consonant (get – getting, swim – swimming, run – running, stop – stopping).

Radio Programmes

Page 36

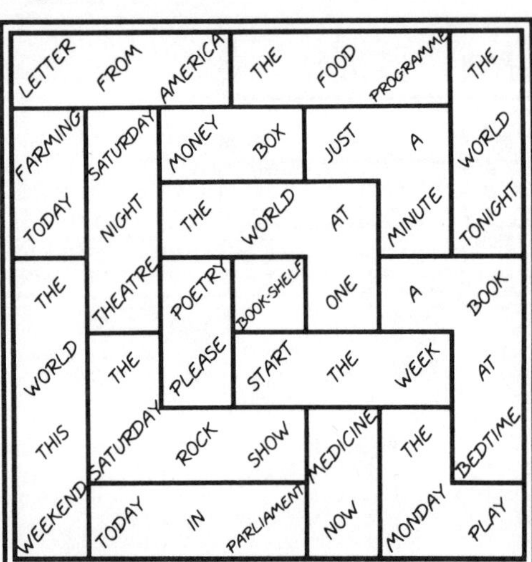

LETTER FROM AMERICA
THE FOOD PROGRAMME
THE WORLD TONIGHT
FARMING TODAY
SATURDAY NIGHT THEATRE
MONEY BOX
JUST A MINUTE
THE WORLD AT ONE
POETRY PLEASE
BOOK-SHELF
A BOOK AT BEDTIME
THE WORLD THIS WEEKEND
THE SATURDAY ROCK SHOW
START THE WEEK
MEDICINE NOW
THE MONDAY PLAY
TODAY IN PARLIAMENT

Fifteen Records

Page 37

is	has	POSSESSIVE
2, 3, 5, 8, 10, 11, 15	6, 12	1, 4, 7, 9, 13, 14

Round and Round

Page 38

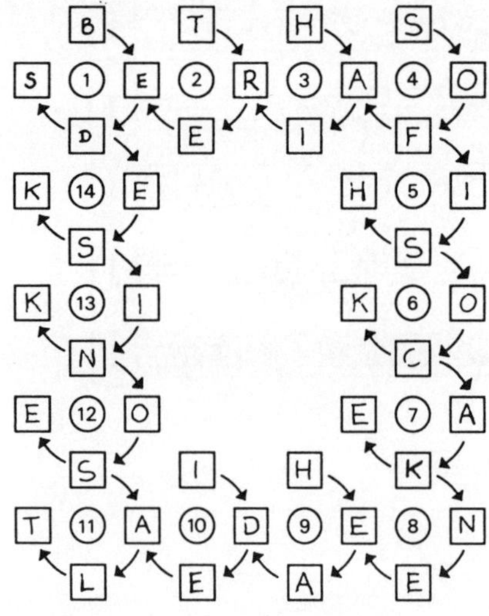

Letters or Words?

Page 39

The letter T sounds like the word tea.
The letter Q sounds like the word queue.
The letter Y sounds like the word why.
The letter U sounds like the word you.
The letter R sounds like the word are.
The letter P sounds like the word pea.
The letter C sounds like the words see and sea.
The letter I sounds like the words eye and I.

1. Be careful!
2. Are you English?
3. seaplane
4. Queue here.
5. teapot
6. See you later.
7. peanuts
8. I'm ill.

Daily Newspapers

Page 40

Daily Express

DAILY
MIRROR

DAILY
STAR

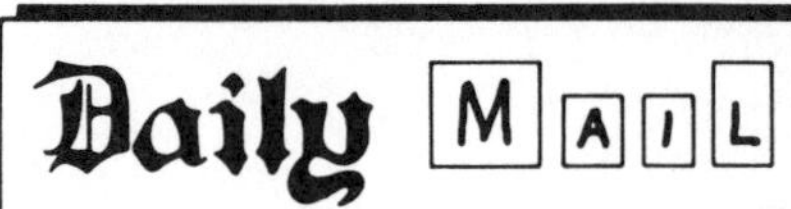

Daily MAIL

Add Three Letters
Page 41

NO	☞	NORTH
TO	☞	TORCH
RED	☞	RECORD
PEN	☞	PENCIL
FAT	☞	FATHER
ICE	☞	POLICE
OTHER	☞	BROTHERS
US	☞	HOUSE
IS	☞	DISCO
GO	☞	GLOVE
BUT	☞	BUTTER
ARE	☞	GARDEN
ONE	☞	ORANGE
TRUE	☞	TRUMPET
THEN	☞	KITCHEN

Rhyming Pairs
Page 42

tea	tree	beer	here
there	chair	hot	what
but	nut	cat	that
put	foot	do	blue
come	some	go	snow
home	Rome	now	how

Olympic Rings
Page 43

Computer Keyboard
Page 44

Q W E R T Y U I O P
A S D F G H J K L
Z X C V B N M

Animals
Page 45

1. lion
2. tortoise
3. chameleon
4. alligator
5. parrot
6. kangaroo
7. rabbit
8. cobra
9. camel
10. spider

Shapes and Letters
Page 46

1. SUN
2. SEA
3. PUT
4. EAST
5. TEA
6. PEN

The word with all seven letters is: PEANUTS

More Newspapers
Page 47

THE TIMES
The Daily Telegraph
THE INDEPENDENT
THE Sun
Today
The Guardian

Radio Stations
Page 48

1. BBC Radio 2
2. BBC Radio 4
3. L.B.C.
4. BBC Radio 3
5. Capital Radio
6. BBC Radio 1
7. G.L.R.

Past and Present
Page 49

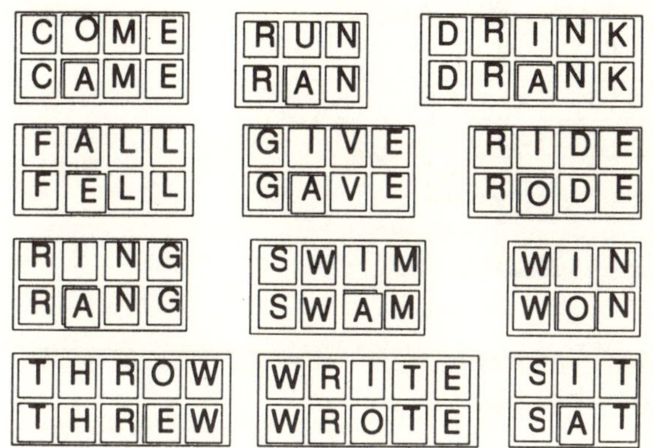
COME
CAME
RUN
RAN
DRINK
DRANK
FALL
FELL
GIVE
GAVE
RIDE
RODE
RING
RANG
SWIM
SWAM
WIN
WON
THROW
THREW
WRITE
WROTE
SIT
SAT

Books, Books, Books
Page 50

A ROOM WITH A VIEW E. M. Forster
THEY CAME TO A CITY J. B. Priestley
TWELFTH NIGHT William Shakespeare
OTHELLO William Shakespeare

LEFT HAND, RIGHT HAND Osbert Sitwell
MAN AND SUPERMAN George Bernard Shaw
ROMEO AND JULIET William Shakespeare
NIGHT AND DAY Virginia Woolf

MEN AND WOMEN Robert Browning
THE SEVEN SEAS Rudyard Kipling
THE SECRET AGENT Joseph Conrad
NINETEEN EIGHTY-FOUR George Orwell

GOODBYE TO BERLIN Christopher Isherwood
THE TIME MACHINE H. G. Wells
STRANGE MEETING Susan Hill
ROBINSON CRUSOE Daniel Defoe

THE GREEN MAN Kingsley Amis
THE THIRD MAN Graham Greene
THE GARDEN PARTY Katherine Mansfield
MR NORRIS CHANGES TRAINS Christopher Isherwood

THE OLD MEN AT THE ZOO Angus Wilson
THE ISLAND Aldous Huxley
THE INVISIBLE MAN H. G. Wells
THE WAR OF THE WORLDS H. G. Wells

Telegrams

Page 51

Telegram One	HAPPY CHRISTMAS!
Telegram Two	HAPPY NEW YEAR!
Telegram Three	HAPPY BIRTHDAY!
Telegram Four	HAPPY TWENTY-FIRST BIRTHDAY!
Telegram Five	WELL DONE! YOU PASSED YOUR DRIVING TEST!
Telegram Six	CONGRATULATIONS! YOU PASSED YOUR EXAM!

Mixed Vegetables

Page 52

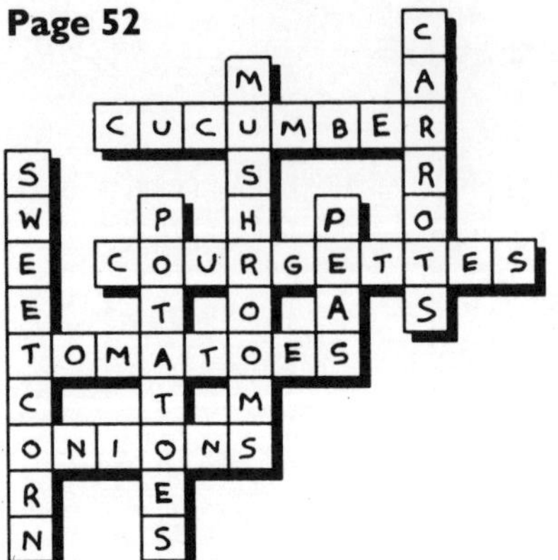

Verb Dice

Page 53

1. STUDIED
2. DANCED
3. PHONED
4. WASHED
5. TYPED
6. PAINTED
7. ARRIVED
8. LISTENED
9. SKATED
10. OPENED

Remember: Most verbs add *ed* (walk*ed*, wash*ed*, paint*ed*, listen*ed*, open*ed*). Verbs ending with a consonant +y use *ied* (study – stud*ied*). Verbs ending with e just add *d* (dance*d*, phone*d*, type*d*, arrive*d*, skate*d*).
Some verbs double the final consonant (stop–stopped).

Record Store

Page 54

1. What is love?
2. Why can't we live together?
3. Who wears these shoes?
4. Where did your heart go?
5. What can I say?
6. How can I be sure?
7. Who am I?
8. Why don't they understand?
9. What is a man?
10. Where do we go from here?
11. Who is it?
12. How can you mend a broken heart?
13. Where are you now?
14. Who are you? (by The Who).

Hidden Prepositions

Page 55

1
WE DIDN'T GO NORTH, WE WENT SOUTH.
2
SUSAN AND JANE ARE SISTERS.
3
WE BOUGHT A NEW SOFA THIS AFTERNOON.
4
THIS WINDOW NEEDS SOME OIL.
5
LET'S VISIT MIAMI NEXT YEAR.
6
IN TIBET WE ENDED OUR JOURNEY.
7
CAN I BORROW A POUND, ERNEST?
8
DID IT RAIN TODAY?

AT
BETWEEN
DOWN
IN
INTO
NEAR
ON
UNDER

The Last Word

Page 56

1. isn't
2. aren't
3. wasn't
4. weren't
5. didn't
6. don't
7. doesn't
8. haven't
9. hasn't
10. can't

Pictures and Opposites

Page 57

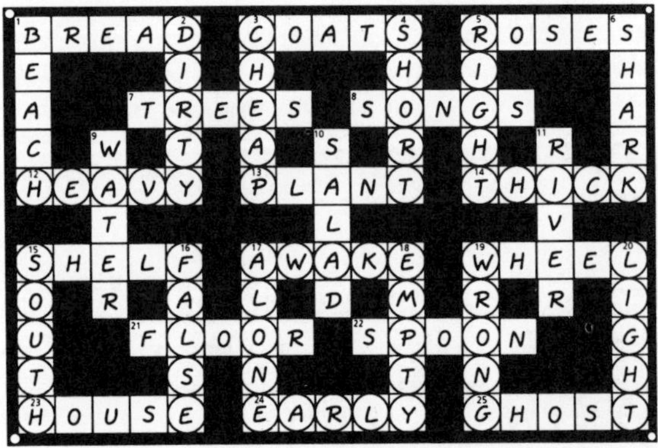

Months Jigsaw

Page 58

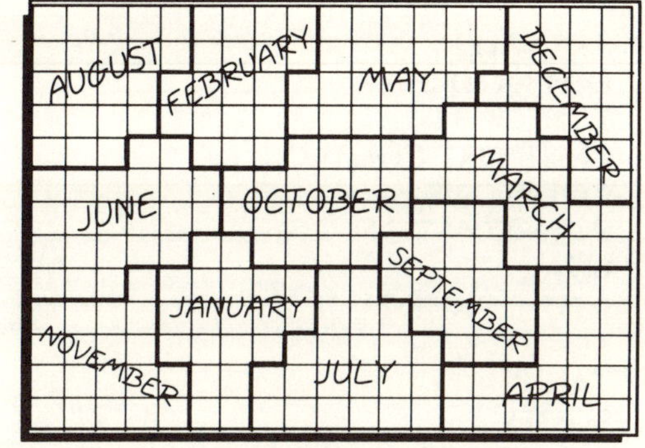
AUGUST
FEBRUARY
MAY
DECEMBER
JUNE
OCTOBER
MARCH
SEPTEMBER
JANUARY
NOVEMBER
JULY
APRIL

Verb Mini-crossword

Page 59

1.

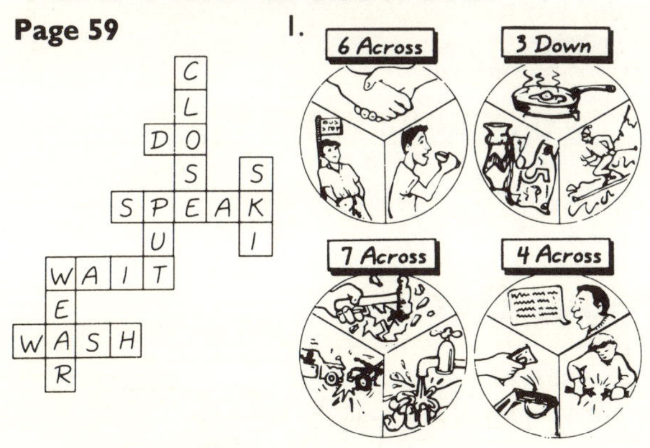
CLOSE
DO
SPEAK
SKI
PUT
WAIT
WEAR
WASH
6 Across
3 Down
7 Across
4 Across

2. Of the six verbs (*lose, close, choose, put, shut, cut*), the two with the same meaning are *close* and *shut*.

Don't Do It – It's Unlucky!

Page 60

6
DON'T WALK UNDER A LADDER
3
DON'T OPEN AN UMBRELLA INDOORS.*
8
DON'T WHISTLE ON A BOAT.
7
DON'T PUT SHOES ON A TABLE.
2
DON'T TALK WHEN YOU ARE UNDER A BRIDGE.
1
DON'T CARRY AN AXE ON YOUR SHOULDER INDOORS.*
4
DON'T GO PAST ANOTHER PERSON ON THE STAIRS.
5
DON'T LOOK BACK WHEN YOU LEAVE YOUR HOME TO GO ON A JOURNEY.

(*The word 'indoors' means 'inside a building'. The opposite is 'outdoors'.)

Calculator

Page 61

(SELL)

(LIE)

(LOSE)

(ILL)

(ELLIE)

(LESLIE)

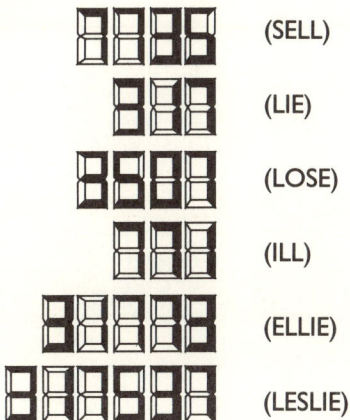

Folding Doors

Page 62

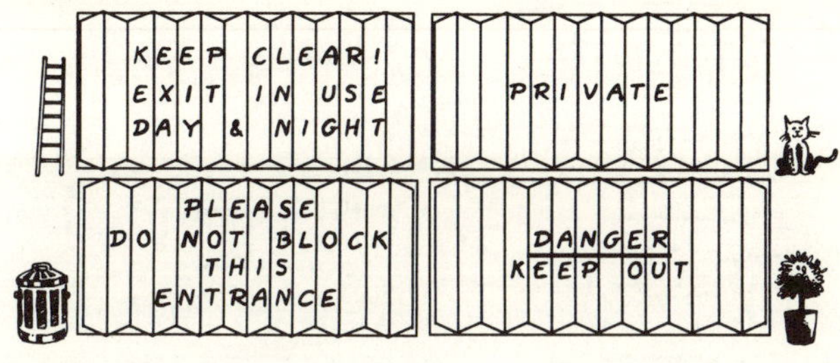
KEEP CLEAR! EXIT IN USE DAY & NIGHT
PRIVATE
PLEASE DO NOT BLOCK THIS ENTRANCE
DANGER KEEP OUT

Longer, Shorter

Page 63

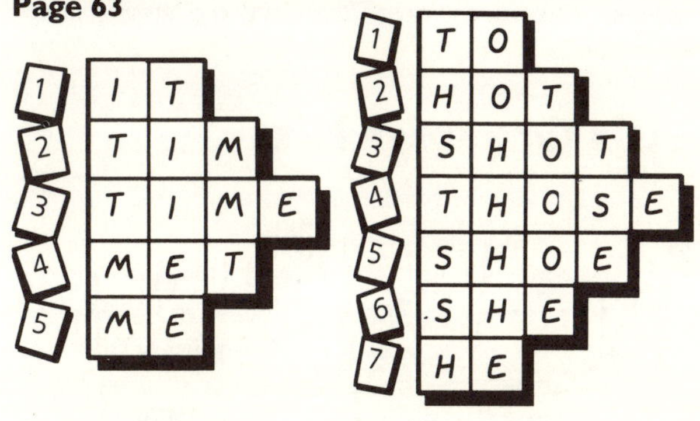
1 IT
2 TIM
3 TIME
4 MET
5 ME
1 TO
2 HOT
3 SHOT
4 THOSE
5 SHOE
6 SHE
7 HE

Identity Parade

Page 64

1. Charles Lindbergh (1902–1974) flew across the Atlantic in 1927, when he was twenty-five years old.
2. Queen Victoria (1819–1901) became Queen of Great Britain and Ireland in 1837, when she was eighteen years old.
3. Napoleon Bonaparte (1769–1821) became Emperor of France in 1804, when he was thirty-five years old.
4. Margaret Thatcher (1925–) became the British Prime Minister in 1979, when she was fifty-three years old.
5. Wolfgang Amadeus Mozart (1756–1791) began composing music in 1761, when he was five years old.
6. Madonna (1959–) made her first record in 1982, when she was twenty-three years old.
7. Pablo Picasso (1881–1973) had his first exhibition in 1901, when he was nineteen years old.

Find the Family

Page 65

1 WEMBLEY STADIUM 2 SYDNEY HARBOUR BRIDGE

3 HADRIAN'S WALL 4 THE TOWER OF LONDON

5 VICTORIA FALLS 6 MOUNT EVEREST

7 THE EIFFEL TOWER

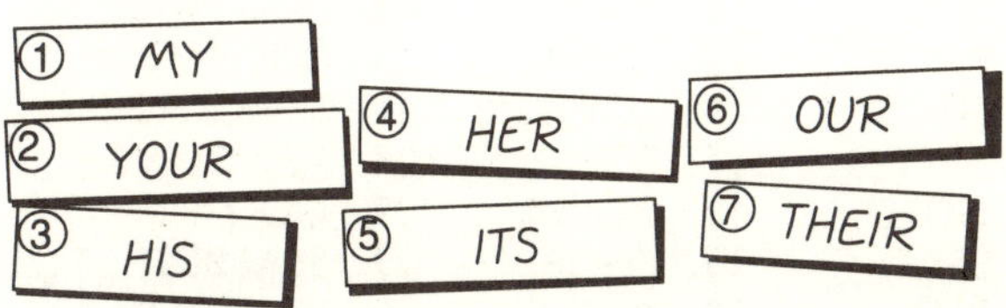
1 MY
2 YOUR
3 HIS
4 HER
5 ITS
6 OUR
7 THEIR

Clothes

Page 66

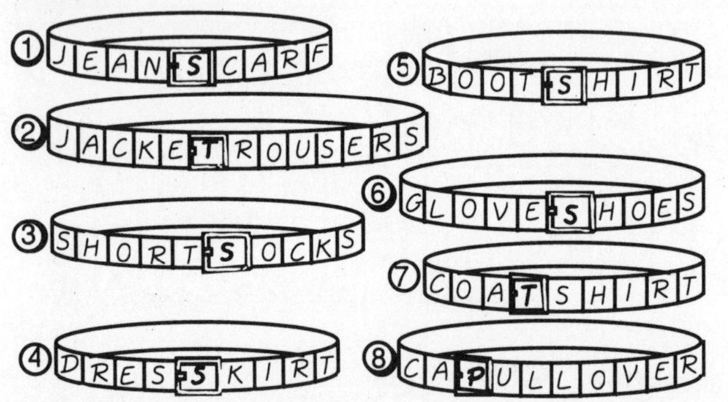

① JEANS SCARF
② JACKET TROUSERS
③ SHORTS SOCKS
④ DRESS SKIRT
⑤ BOOTS SHIRT
⑥ GLOVES SHOES
⑦ COAT T-SHIRT
⑧ CAP PULLOVER

Remember: The words 'jeans', 'trousers' and 'shorts' are always plural.

Elvis's Greatest Hits

Page 67

GUITAR KENTUCKY LITTLE LOVE ONE TEDDY WOODEN
BEAR HEART LETTERS MAN RAIN NIGHT SISTER
LOVE LETTERS
KENTUCKY RAIN
GUITAR MAN
TEDDY BEAR
ONE NIGHT
LITTLE SISTER
WOODEN HEART
a b c d e f g h i j k l m
1 WOODEN HEART
2 ONE NIGHT
3 LOVE LETTERS
4 KENTUCKY RAIN
5 GUITAR MAN
6 TEDDY BEAR
7 LITTLE SISTER
6g 3a 5b 2c BLUE 5h 3b 1c 4m MOON
6g 7e 4e 6b BLUE 6j 2f 3c 7f 3k RIVER
6g 3f 5b 3j BLUE 4f 2h 1k 5c 7j 3i 5h 1j 3l CHRISTMAS

(The word 'blue' is a colour, but it can also mean 'sad'.)

A+B=C

Page 68

1. TOOTH	11. BALL	21. TOOTHBRUSH
2. HAND	12. BOY	22. HANDBAG
3. SUN	13. BRUSH	23. SUNFLOWER
4. FOOT	14. BELT	24. FOOTBALL
5. BOOK	15. CHAIR	25. BOOKSHOP
6. SCHOOL	16. FLOWER	26. SCHOOLBOY
7. ARM	17. FISH	27. ARMCHAIR
8. GOLD	18. ROOM	28. GOLDFISH
9. SEAT	19. SHOP	29. SEATBELT
10. BED	20. BAG	30. BEDROOM

Mistakes at the Airport

Page 69

1. ARRIVAL~~L~~S — L
2. DEP~~P~~ARTURES — P
3. ~~T~~CHECK-IN — T
4. PASS~~E~~PORT CONTROL — E
5. C~~O~~USTOMS — O
6. INFOR~~D~~MATION — D
7. B~~H~~AR — H
8. RESTAURA~~U~~NT — U
9. TOILET~~T~~S — T
10. TAXI~~Y~~S — Y
11. BUS~~S~~ES — S
12. NO SMOK~~E~~ING — E
13. MEN~~N~~ — N
14. CAR~~R~~ PARK — R
15. W~~H~~OMEN — H
16. OUT OF~~F~~ ORDER — F

ONE MORE PLACE :

6	8	9	10		16	14	4	12		11	7	5	2
D	U	T	Y	-	F	R	E	E	■	S	H	O	P

Famous Dates

Page 70

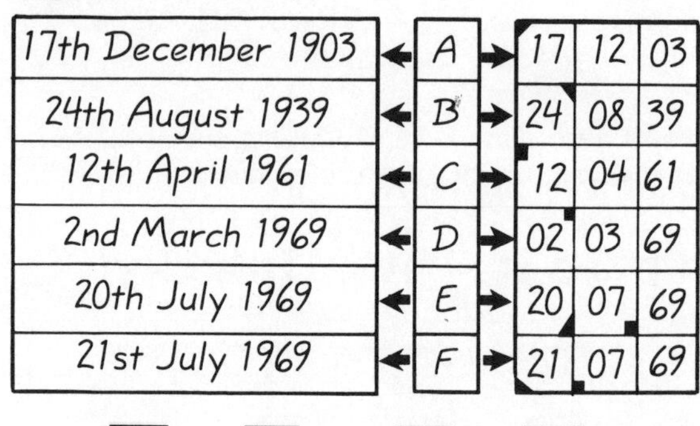

17th December 1903 A 17 12 03
24th August 1939 B 24 08 39
12th April 1961 C 12 04 61
2nd March 1969 D 02 03 69
20th July 1969 E 20 07 69
21st July 1969 F 21 07 69

12 + 02 = 07 + 07 **(14)**

17 + 24 = 20 + 21 **(41)**

Note: The dates in numbers (e.g. 17.12.03) are in the British style: day, month, year. In the United States, a different order is used: month, day, year (e.g. 12.17.03).

Longer, Shorter, Longer . . .

Page 71

1	IN	15	MEAT
2	TIN	16	METAL
3	TINA	17	LATE
4	TRAIN	18	TEA
5	RAIN	19	AT
6	RAN	20	SAT
7	AN	21	SALT
8	MAN	22	TAILS
9	MEAN	23	LIST
10	NAMES	24	SIT
11	SAME	25	IS
12	SAM	26	HIS
13	AM	27	THIS
14	MAT	28	SHIRT